Corvette

America's Sports Car

pil

Publications International, Ltd.

Louis Weber, CEO
Publications International, Ltd.
8140 Lehigh Avenue
Morton Grove, IL 60053

ISBN: 978-1-64558-261-8

Manufactured in China.

8 7 6 5 4 3 2 1

The editors gratefully acknowledge those who supplied photography for this book:

Mark Bilek; Chevrolet Division of General Motors Company; Mitch Frumkin; Thomas Glatch; Sam Griffith; Bud Juneau; Dan Lyons; Vince Manocchi; Doug Mitchel; Neil Nissing; Nina Padgett-Russin; Jeff Rose; Phil Toy; W.C. Waymack; Nicky Wright.

Special thanks to the owners of the featured cars, without whose enthusiastic cooperation this book would not have been possible.

Thanks also to Chevrolet Public Relations; GM Photographic; Lockheed Martin; Wieck Media Services.

CONTENTS

CHAPTER 1

MOTORAMA CORVETTE

A booming postwar economy had injected vigor and vitality into the automotive business, and, in response to their growing popularity, Detroit finally began to take sports cars seriously. In the early 1950s, a handful of foresighted individuals at General Motors pioneered a new concept car that would bring an enthusiast's dream to reality, and give birth to an automotive legend.

Introduced in January 1953 at New York's Waldorf-Astoria Hotel, the Corvette Motorama show car was greeted with great enthusiasm, and went into production a few months later with only minor changes.

Harley J. Earl (opposite page, left) founded General Motors' Art and Colour Section in the mid 1930s, making it the American auto industry's first in-house styling department. He virtually invented the "dream car" concept with his Buick Y-Job show car of 1938. Inspired by the racy postwar sports cars of Europe, Earl designed the Corvette in secret and pushed it through as his pet project. Chassis engineer Robert F. McLean placed the engine behind the front axle rather than over it to improve front/rear weight distribution. In the interest of cost, most chassis and driveline components were off-the-shelf Chevy components.

Ed Cole (center) was Chevrolet's chief engineer when the Motorama Corvette was revealed. He spearheaded work on the company's fabulous small-block V-8 that arrived for 1955, which helped transform the Corvette into a true sports car. Further transformation came at the hands of race driver and Chevrolet engineer Zora Arkus-Duntov (right) who improved the Corvette's handling and was eventually appointed the car's chief engineer. Known as "Mr. Corvette," Duntov guided the car's development for nearly 20 years, and remained involved even after his retirement.

The Motorama Corvette (foreground) sat noticeably lower than Chevrolet's full-size 1953 model (background). Changes to production versions were slight. Most noticeable were the deletion of the small scoops just forward of the windshield pillars, removal of the Corvette script below the hood badge, and the substitution of longer chrome side trim with its "wing" turned up instead of down. Then as today, it was nearly unheard of that a show car would make it to production with so few alterations.

C1

1953–1962

PART 1: 1953–1955

Buoyed by a wildly enthusiastic introduction as a concept car at GM's 1953 Motorama, company executives put production of the Corvette on a fast track. But the cars proved difficult to build, and lukewarm reviews combined with lackluster sales threatened to bench the Corvette before it could reach its stride.

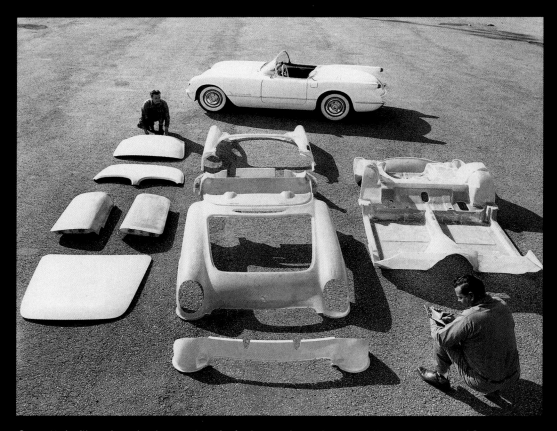

Corvette's fiberglass body consisted of nine major subassemblies made from 46 separate pieces. The art of fiberglass construction was in its infancy at General Motors, and early cars were built by hand since a lot of detail work was required to get everything to fit properly. Nevertheless, the first production model was driven off the assembly line on June 30, 1953, just six months after the Corvette's public unveiling as a Motorama show car.

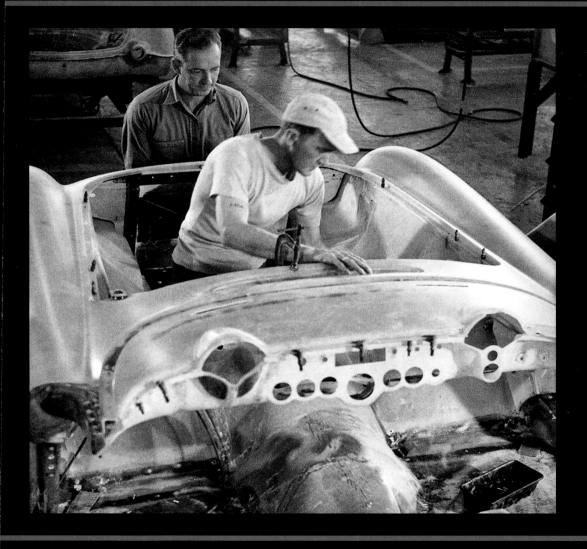

All 1953 Corvettes were painted white, and fitted with a red interior and black folding top. Early models wore smooth-center wheel covers as shown here; later '53s and all '54s were fitted with sculpted covers similar to those used on the Motorama show car. The engine was Chevy's stodgy old 235-cubic-inch six, but triple carburetors and other modifications boosted horsepower from 105 to 150. The only transmission was a two-speed automatic, a sore point with sports car traditionalists, who preferred manuals. Yet despite the rather mundane mechanicals, a Corvette was quite fast for its day, as a well-tuned example could do 0-to-60 mph in 11 seconds and hit 105 mph flat out.

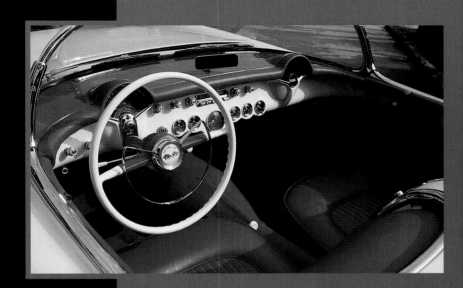

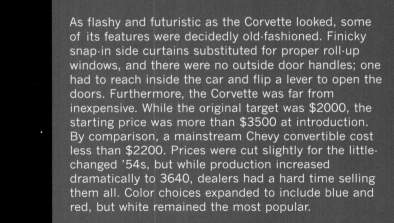

As flashy and futuristic as the Corvette looked, some of its features were decidedly old-fashioned. Finicky snap-in side curtains substituted for proper roll-up windows, and there were no outside door handles; one had to reach inside the car and flip a lever to open the doors. Furthermore, the Corvette was far from inexpensive. While the original target was $2000, the starting price was more than $3500 at introduction. By comparison, a mainstream Chevy convertible cost less than $2200. Prices were cut slightly for the little-changed '54s, but while production increased dramatically to 3640, dealers had a hard time selling them all. Color choices expanded to include blue and red, but white remained the most popular.

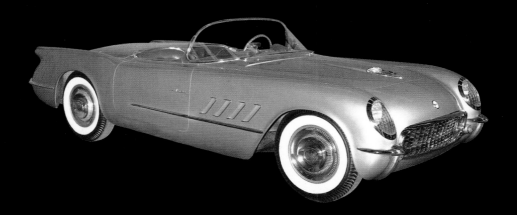

Opposite page: A trio of Corvette variants appeared at the 1954 Motorama show. One wore a removable hardtop that would appear for 1956, a wagon called Nomad would inspire a similar 1955 full-size Chevy production car, and a fastback version foretold the Stingray coupe that would arrive for 1963. *This page:* Minor design changes were proposed for 1955 but shelved due to slow sales.

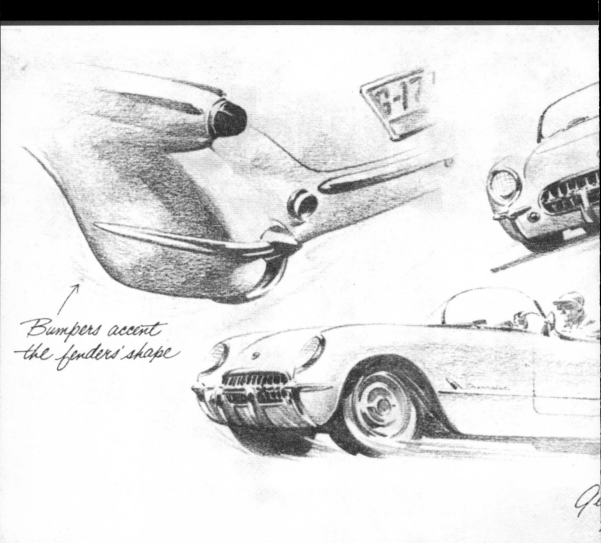

Bumpers accent
the fenders' shape

fiber-plastic body

terrific impact

resistance

"Loaded for bear"

There's mighty potent ammunition under the hood of the new Corvette—for now the "Blue-Flame" 6 is joined by a very special 195-h.p. version of the astonishing Chevrolet V8 engine!

This is the engine sports car drivers have been waiting for—compact, low in weight, ultra-rigid, with all the inherent virtues of Chevrolet's three-inch stroke, massive crankshaft, and short manifolds. And when you add an almost pressure-free dual exhaust system, a high-lift camshaft and four-barrel carburetor, you get *GO* in great big capital letters!

How does it go? Like "The Ride of the Valkyries," the takeoff of a V-2 rocket, the plunge down the Cresta bobsled run—all wrapped up in one! You *never* felt anything like this sheer triumphant surge of power ... or the way the V8 Corvette cruises, as effortlessly as a flame burns.

Even if you have known the Corvette before ... if you have tested its rock-solid

stability on curves, its polo-pony compactness, its fantastic grip on the road, and its hairline 16 to 1 steering ... the V8 version will stun you. But if you have never driven any Corvette, then you are to be envied. You have an experience coming—a singing jubilation that will tingle in your memory all the rest of your life!

True, you risk spoiling yourself for every other kind of car. But why not phone your Chevrolet dealer, now, and set up a date with the new V8? ... Chevrolet Division of General Motors, Detroit 2, Michigan.

 CHEVROLET CORVETTE

Corvettes got a major boost for 1955 with the arrival of Chevrolet's new 265-cubic-inch V-8. Rated at 195 horsepower, it put out 40 more than Corvette's standard six-cylinder. Late in the model year a three-speed manual transmission was offered, and with that, the Corvette could finally be called a true sports car.

As might be expected, the new V-8 made a huge difference in Corvette's performance.

The 0-to-60-mph sprint now took just 8.5 seconds (vs. 11.0), and top speed rose from 105 mph to nearly 120.

All but six of the 674 Corvettes built for 1955 carried the new V-8, signified by an exaggerated gold "V" in the chrome name script behind the front wheelwell. The substantial drop in sales was largely due to the introduction of Ford's Thunderbird, which cost nearly the same but included far more amenities—and outsold the Corvette by a ratio of 23 to 1.

Corvette's symmetrical dashboard certainly looked the part of a sporting machine, but critics bemoaned the fact that many of the gauges were positioned low and far from the driver's line of sight—particularly the centrally mounted tachometer.

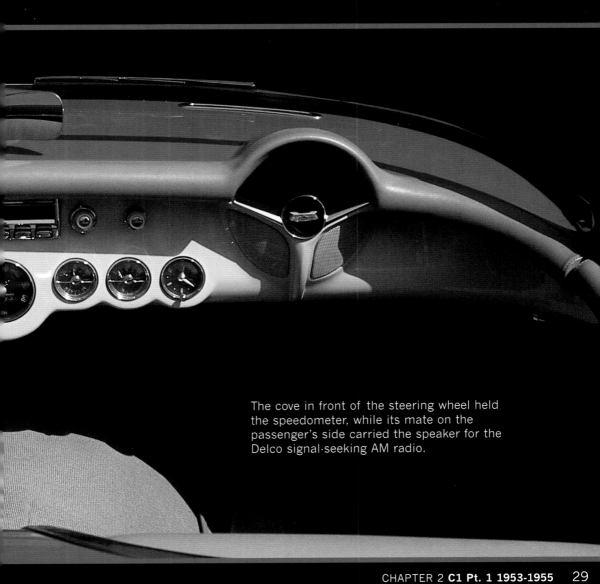

The cove in front of the steering wheel held the speedometer, while its mate on the passenger's side carried the speaker for the Delco signal-seeking AM radio.

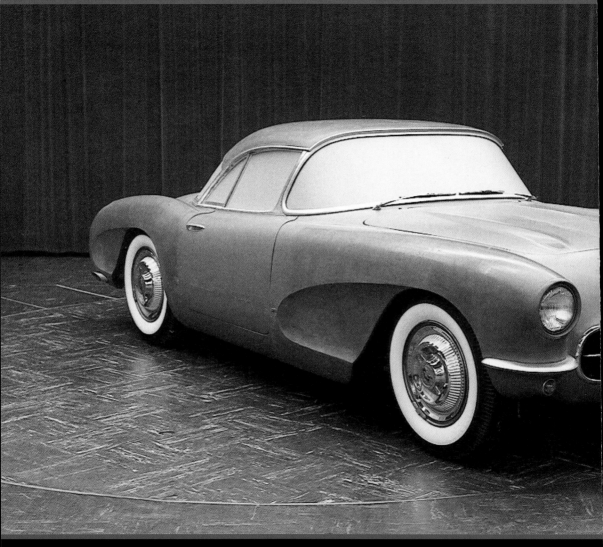

Sculpted side coves would grace a revised 1956 Corvette. Styling studies from February 1955 show the coves were already being considered—both front and rear. Final styling wasn't locked up until May '55, just a few months before the car's introduction.

C1

1953–1962

PART 2: 1956–1957

With sales at a fraction of expectations, Corvette would require major surgery to avoid an early demise. Fortunately, Harley Earl and company had just what the doctor ordered, and the results turned heads, scorched racetracks, and produced among the most collectible of all Corvettes.

A NEW CORVETTE
BY CHEVROLET

Now

greater than the original in . . .

Looks and Performance!

A dismal 1955 selling season all but killed Chevrolet's fledgling sports car. Something spectacular would have to happen if it were to survive. Fortunately, something did. Born anew for 1956, the Corvette boasted fresh, exciting styling and even more power from its now-standard V-8 engine. Furthermore, expected conveniences such as roll-up windows and outside door handles were added with only a slight increase in price. Buyers responded, sales jumped more than fivefold, and the Corvette was saved.

While fiberglass was tricky to work with, it didn't require the huge, expensive presses demanded by conventional steel bodies, making styling changes less expensive—something that worked in Corvette's favor. Shorn of its gimmicky tailfins, the car took on a more serious sporting look, an impression backed up by a newly standard three-speed manual transmission and 210-horsepower V-8.

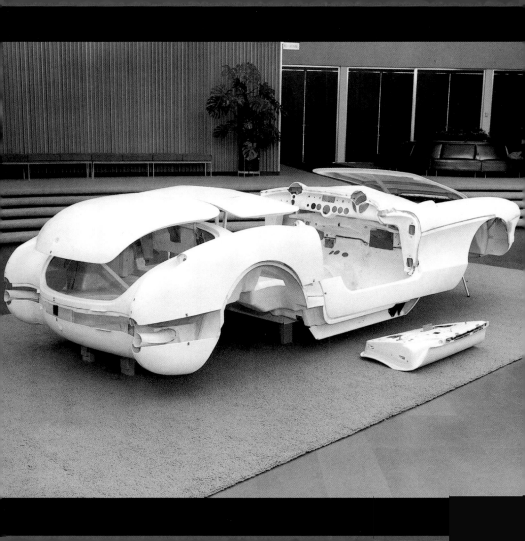

Close-up details reveal *new* Corvette Advancements

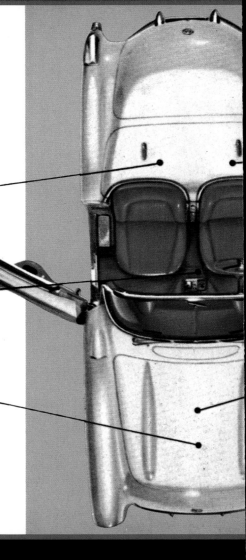

A touch . . . and she's up!

A new fabric top power mechanism, optional at extra cost, automatically raises the top or folds it out of sight under its covered compartment. Wider rear windows and new-design side windows increase visibility.

This . . . is for the "Box Boys"

The new Corvette has a new floor-mounted manual shift and new close ratio Synchro-Mesh transmission. Here is the split-second up-shifting, down-shifting, close-ratio gear control demanded by the experts!

Eight-Jet Carburetion for take-offs!

The Corvette's 265-cubic-inch V8 engine owes its great horsepower to twin 4-barrel carburetion (optional at extra cost), higher compression ratio and new manifolds with twin pipe exhausts.

Avant-Garde styling with a touch of tradition

The Corvette is a true sports car—not a scaled-down convertible. Now it's even more adventurous looking with graceful new fender lines, new side panel and hood treatment, and simulated knock-off type wheel covers.

Quick change! A roadster or coupe!

A smart plastic hardtop, richly trimmed with bright metal and featuring a wrap-around rear window for greater visibility, enhances Corvette's versatile styling. It is easily installed or removed.

Let it rain, let it snow!

Corvette offers the convenience of roll-up regulators that quickly raise and lower the new windows. Power window lifts are available as an extra-cost option.

A hood full of "Horses" add a carload of Safety!

The new Corvette V8 engine is a real lifesaver when only sheer *passing power* can leave hazards behind and whisk you to safety. New cylinder heads raise Corvette's compression ratio to 9.25 to 1!

"Out-front" styling for looking ahead

The raised-forward portion of the fender houses an improved design headlight that projects forward to extend the fender-line and contribute to Corvette's rakish look.

Brochures were quick to point out Corvette's new features. Now it was not only a serious sports car, but one you could easily live with.

Aside from the newly rounded tail, perhaps Corvette's most prominent design feature was a side cove that tapered back from the front wheelwell. For a slight extra fee, it could be painted in a contrasting color. Also new for '56—and also at extra cost—was a removable hardtop. Other options included power windows, power-operated top, and a leading-edge transistorized signal-seeking radio.

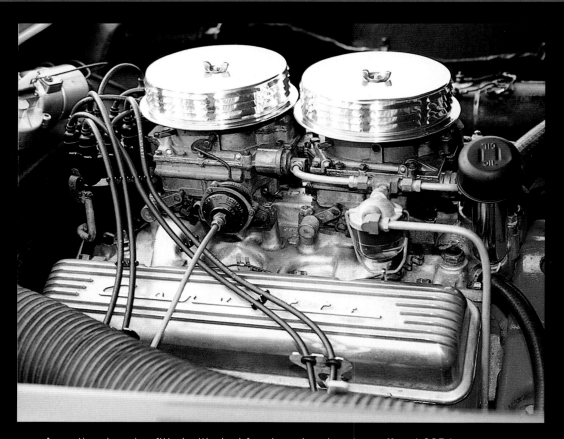

An optional engine fitted with dual four-barrel carburetors offered 225 horsepower. Also available for that engine was a special high-lift cam developed by Duntov, but the combination carried no advertised power rating. *Opposite page:* Despite all the changes outside, there were few alterations to interior decor other than the substitution of a sporty three-spoke steering wheel.

283 **CUBIC INCHES**

283 **HORSEPOWER**

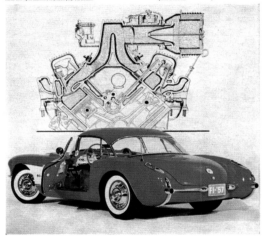

TOWARD AN AMERICAN CLASSIC . . . THE 1957 CORVETTE WITH FUEL INJECTION! It is with considerable pride that Chevrolet invites you to examine an engineering advance of great significance, available on the 1957 Corvette. It is fuel injection, and in the Corvette V8 it permits a level of efficiency hitherto unrealized in any American production car: *one horsepower for every cubic inch of displacement . . . 283 h.p.!* In addition, there is unprecedented responsiveness, even during warm-up; virtually instantaneous acceleration and significant gains in overall gas economy.

This is another major step in the creation of a proud new kind of car for America: a *genuine* sports car, as certified by its record in competition. But a *unique* sports car in its combination of moderate price, luxurious equipment and low-cost maintenance with fiery performance, polo-pony responsiveness and granite stability on curves.

It is our intention to make of the Corvette a classic car, one of those rare and happy milestones in the history of automotive design. We take pleasure in inviting you to drive the 1957 version—and see just how close we have come to the target. . . . *Chevrolet Division of General Motors, Detroit 2, Michigan.*

SPECIFICATIONS: 283-cubic-inch V8 engine with single four-barrel carburetor, 220 h.p. (four other engines* range to 283 h.p. with fuel injection). Close-ratio three-speed manual transmission standard, with special Powerglide automatic drive* available on all but maximum-performance engines. Choice of removable hard top or power-operated fabric top, Power-Lift windows.* Instruments include 6000 r.p.m. tachometer, oil pressure gauge and ammeter. *Optional at extra cost.

CORVETTE

by Chevrolet

For 1957, Chevrolet fitted fuel injection to an enlarged 283-cubic-inch V-8 and got 283 horsepower—the magical one horsepower per cubic inch. Though it was not the first engine with fuel injection—or the first to make one horsepower per cubic inch—it was quite exotic for the time. Today, a '57 "fuelie" is among the most coveted of Corvettes.

CHEVROLET'S
NEW **CORVETTE**

"REALLY, OLD BOY, YOU AREN'T SUPPOSED TO BUILD THAT SORT OF THING IN AMERICA, Y'KNOW."

The unforgivable thing, of course, is this: The new Corvette not only looks delightful and rides like the Blue Train—but it also is quite capable of macerating the competition out on the road circuits.

This dual nature is the classic requirement before you can call a pretty two-seater a *sports car*. And properly so, for this is an honorable name, and only a vehicle with race-bred precision of handling, cornering and control can make a mortal driver feel quite so akin to the gods.

Unlike the gentleman above, who has been a little slow in catching up with current events, most sports car people are becoming aware that the Corvette is truly one of the world's most remarkable cars. Because it does two disparate things outstandingly well: It provides superbly practical motoring, with every luxury and convenience your heart might covet, and accompanies this with a soul-satisfying ferocity of performance.

We could recite the full specifications. But if you are the kind of driver who is meant for a Corvette, you'll want to find out firsthand—and that, sir, would be our pleasure! . . . *Chevrolet Division of General Motors, Detroit 2, Michigan.*

SPECIFICATIONS: 283-cubic-inch V8 engine with single four-barrel carburetor, 230 h.p. (four other engines* range to 283 h.p. with fuel injection). Close-ratio three-speed manual transmission standard, with special Powerglide automatic drive* available on all fuel injection-performance engines. Choice of removable hard top or power-operated fabric top, Power-Lift windows.* Instruments include 6000 r.p.m. tachometer, oil pressure gauge and ammeter. *Optional at extra cost.

CORVETTE
by Chevrolet

There's a groove in every curve... for Corvettes!

Well, that's what it *feels* like! And that feeling—the solid road-gripping security, the superb sense of control and command—is something that only the genuine sports car can give you.

What's the feeling worth? Very little, if you're not much interested in driving for its own sake. But if you are, nothing man has ever built can produce the same dazzling surge of delight!

Seriously, here's a test you should try if you want to know just how much pure pleasure you can pack into motoring: Borrow a Corvette, pick a stretch of wickedly curving road that you really respect—and cruise into it. Surprise! What happened to the bends that used to set the tail wagging, the car drifting out toward the center line, the body tilting? Sure, they're the same curves—but this is the way a car ought to go round them. Flat, locked in its own lane, riding the radius as though in an invisible groove!

What *kind* of a Corvette should you choose for this test? Any one, from the expert's version with fuel injection V8* and four-speed gearbox* to the butter-smooth Powerglide* town car. There are all sorts of engine, transmission and luxury equipment options. But we make only one kind of chassis—the honest-to-Pete sports car kind, with road-holding no other car in America can match! Try it—and see what it feels like to find a groove in every curve! . . . *Chevrolet Division of General Motors, Detroit 2, Mich.* *Optional at extra cost.

CORVETTE
by Chevrolet

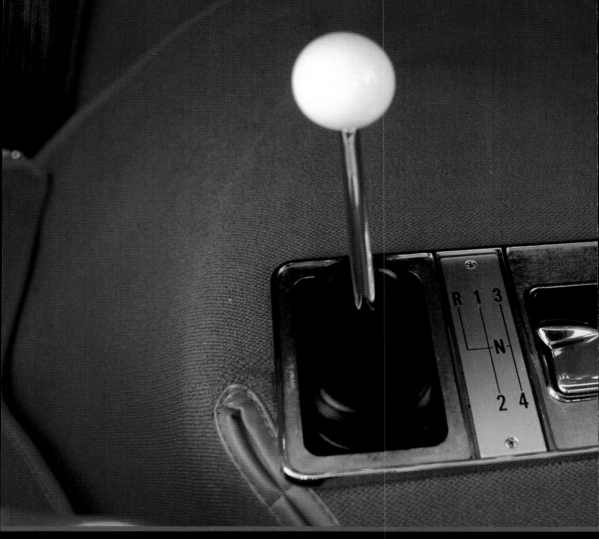

Also added for 1957 was an optional four-speed manual transmission. When combined with the new fuel-injected engine, a Corvette so equipped could do 0-60 mph in just 5.7 seconds. The car pictured has both features—along with simple "dog dish" hubcaps. If ever there was a "sleeper" Corvette, this was it.

Right: Developed for racing, the SR-2 was based on a 1956 Corvette. Fitted with aerodynamic aids including a tapered nose, cut-down windshields, and a flared headrest, it met with mild success. A 1957 update (top row) added headlight domes and a larger headrest fairing. *Opposite, bottom:* Another Corvette-based special was the Super Sport show car, with "double bubble" windshield, bisecting racing stripe, and small scoops in the bodyside coves, à la the SR-2.

A desire to win the prestigious 12 Hours of Sebring prompted Chevrolet to build the aptly named Sebring SS for the 1957 race. While stock Corvettes were quite successful in competition, they couldn't hope to compete with the purpose-built racers from Europe for an overall win. Though styled with several Corvette cues—such as side coves and toothy grille—the Sebring SS didn't share much with its street-going brethren aside from the basic 283-cubic-inch engine block soon to be fitted to '57 'Vettes.

While it proved competitive, its racing life was brief: Suspension problems sidelined it on the 23rd lap, and due to an industry-sponsored racing ban imposed shortly thereafter, the SS never competed again. However, it later appeared as a GM show car, and in 1959, lapped the new Daytona International Speedway at an amazing 183 mph.

C1

1953–1962

PART 3: 1958–1962

Styling revisions fore and aft along with ever-increasing power kept the Corvette fresh and its sales climbing through the end of its first generation.

Chevrolet

CORVETTE

1958

Nearly all American cars adopted quad headlights for 1958, and the Corvette was no exception. In addition, pronounced "nostrals" flanked the grille, and louvers appeared between the hood's twin windsplits. Ads continued to promote the 'Vettes performance prowess along with its "International" appeal.

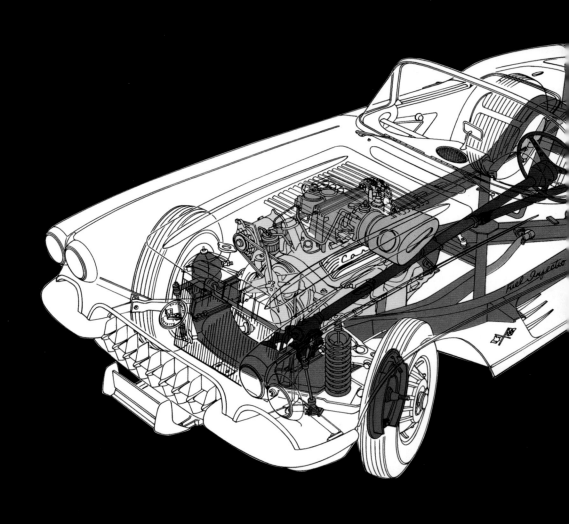

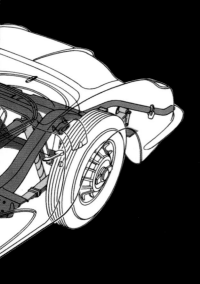

Underneath, the Corvette was little-changed, still with a solid rear axle held by leaf springs. Engines remained at 283 cubic inches, but now ranged from 230 horsepower to 290—up a few from '57. Most appreciated, however, was the new dashboard A twin-cove design grouped all gauges squarely in front of the driver, a big improvement over the spread-out style of the earlier layout.

Corvette's faired-in taillight coves gained streamlined lenses for '58, the only year the trunklid bore twin chrome spears; like the hood louvers, the spears were discarded during a 1959 housecleaning. As it had since Day One, the convertible top retracted beneath a sleek form-fitting cover.

CORVETTE, '59 EDITION
by Chevrolet

NEW SLEEKNESS, ELEGANCE AND ROADABILITY FOR AMERICA'S ONLY SPORTS CAR!

Take a great basic design. Give its creators time to polish and refine every facet of its behavior—and you can come up with a classic road machine like the new Corvette.

Every change made for 1959 contributes new precision, new performance, new pleasure to what is admittedly the greatest driver's car produced in this country. Everything, from the superior traction of the new rear suspension to the deeper "bucket" contour of the seats to the cooling air slots in the wheel discs, is designed from the pilot's point of view.

Corvette, quite literally, offers a completely different dimension in road travel. If you haven't driven any Corvette yet, we can promise you a genuinely astonishing afternoon. But, even if you have experienced earlier versions, even if you are now a Corvette owner, we urge this: Try the '59 edition—you, too, can be profoundly impressed! . . . Chevrolet Division of General Motors, Detroit 2, Michigan.

Shorn of the hood louvers and chrome trunk spears, the '59 Corvette was a tidier ship. Ads made it sound as though it would make a splendid addition to anyone's garage—a point this fine '59 makes difficult to argue.

Corvette's top fuel-injected engine got a boost to 315 horsepower for 1960, but the car got an even bigger boost from George Maharis (left) and Martin Milner, who drove a new 'Vette from one adventure to the next on TV's *Route 66*. The popular show lasted into 1964, with Maharis eventually being replaced by Glenn Corbett. The show debuted in 1960, the first year Corvette sales topped 10,000 units. Coincidence?

An early styling study (opposite, top) forecast a "tail lift" given the Corvette for 1961. The update also brought a mesh grille to replace the former toothy grin, but the proposed vertical cove vents and circular grille badge didn't make the cut.

corvette
FOR 1962

Marking the end of the C1 generation of Corvettes was the 1962 edition, which featured a surprising number of changes for a close-out model. The grille went to black, bright ribbed rocker-panel trim was added, and the side-cove vents switched from chrome spears to simple vanes. And for the first time since their introduction on the '56 model, the coves couldn't wear a contrasting color. Inset: Never again would Corvette buyers see a trunk this roomy and accessible.

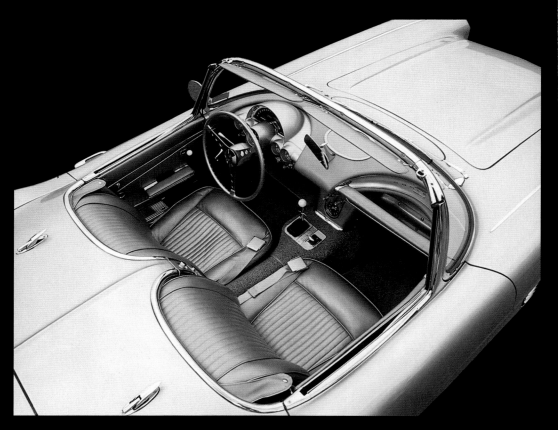

Aside from the styling changes, perhaps the biggest news for '62 was an enlarged 327-cubic-inch V-8 that produced up to 360 horsepower in fuel-injected form—a heady 45-hp increase over the top '61 fuelie. The C1 generation is often referred to as the "solid-axle Corvettes," since subsequent models would all use independent rear suspension.

CHAPTER 3

C2

1963–1967

With sales going nowhere but up, Chevrolet boldly ushered in a radically new Corvette that was again based on a show car, which itself was based on a racer. This dual parentage paid dividends in both styling and performance, and sales continued their upward trend.

Despite the fact Corvette sales continued to climb, Chevrolet approved a complete redesign for 1963. Based on styling chief Bill Mitchell's Stingray racer of the late '50s (top row and right), it carried creased wheelwell arches and beltline along with tapered nose and tail. An enclosed version was added and made it to production as the famed "split-window coupe" (bottom row).

NEW CORVETTE

New indeed was the '63 Corvette, which added "Sting Ray" to its name as evidenced on the decklid badge. Even the chassis was significantly altered with the adoption of independent rear suspension. Only powertrains were carried over, the top engine option again being a fuel-injected 360-horsepower 327 V-8. This brochure cover depicts the newest of the new, Corvette's first-ever coupe. It was referred to as the "split window" due to the spine that ran through the rear glass. Though it compromised visibility, stylist Bill Mitchell insisted it was essential to the overall design. Nevertheless, it lasted only one year before being removed, making a '63 Corvette coupe easy to spot. Perhaps in deference to the new enclosed model, air conditioning was offered for the first time.

Another unique element of the '63 design was the twin air vents on the hood, which, like the split window, were removed the following year. Unlike the window, however, the simulated vents were fitted to both coupes and convertibles, making it easy to identify any '63 from the front.

A '63 brochure showed the Corvette in all possible body configurations, including a convertible with optional hardtop (lower right). The new design incorporated a revised dashboard, which retained the twin cowls and driver-focused instruments but with a more modern look.

From virtually any angle, the '63 'Vette was one sharp-looking car. Buyers evidently agreed, as sales topped 21,000 units, a near 50 percent increase. Just over half were convertibles, which started at $4037, nearly identical to the '62 price. Oddly, the coupe cost more—by about $200.

Optional on fuel-injected Sting Rays was the Z06 competition package, which included heavy-duty brakes and suspension along with a 36.5-gallon fuel tank. It was also supposed to include nifty aluminum knock-off wheels, but due to quality problems, it's doubtful any cars left the factory with them. However, many 'Vettes were retrofitted when the wheels became available the following year.

GM styling chief Bill Mitchell customized a new '63 convertible as a gift to his predecessor, Harley Earl. Features included a leather-lined cockpit with extra gauges, a hopped-up 327 V-8 with prominent side exhaust pipes, plus special paint with central racing stripe. If only *all* presents could be this cool.

In defiance of the American Manufacturers Association 1957 racing ban, Duntov surreptitiously built five Corvette-based Grand Sports for competition. The cars met with a fair degree of success, but development was ultimately halted by Chevrolet management. All five survive today. One version featured an aluminum-block 377-cubic-inch V-8 with four Weber sidedraft carburetors.

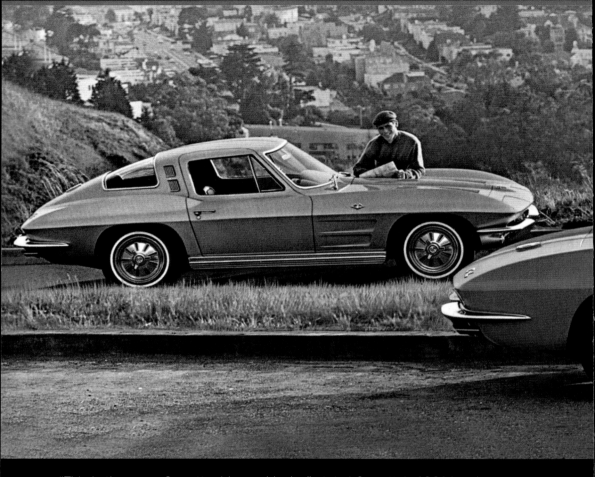

"This is the way a Corvette rides and looks," stated Corvette's 1964 brochure, depicting the cars overlooking an Italian countryside in a not-so-subtle attempt to associate them with such exotics as Ferrari and Lamborghini.

Also mentioned was the 'Vette's new one-piece rear window (for "great hindsight") and ventless hood "with clean, uncluttered surfaces." Corvettes also got some chassis revisions for '64, and the top 327 fuelie was boosted to 375 horsepower.

Aluminum Wide-Rim Wheels* with Knock-off Hubs

| CORVETTE POWER TEAMS | | | | | | Rear Axle Ratio | |
HP	Induction System	Comp. Ratio	Cam Lifters	Distributor Points, Advance	Trans-mission	Std.	*Posi-traction
250	4-Barrel Carburetor, Dual-Intake Air Cleaner	10.5:1	Std. Cam, Hydraulic Lifters	Single, Vacuum-Centrifugal	3-Speed	3.36:1	3.36:1
					4-Speed* (2.56:1 Low)	3.36:1†	3.36:1
					Powerglide*	3.36:1	3.36:1
300*	Large 4-Barrel Carburetor, Dual-Intake Air Cleaner	10.5:1	Std. Cam, Hydraulic Lifters	Single, Vacuum-Centrifugal	3-Speed	3.36:1	3.36:1
					4-Speed* (2.56:1 Low)	3.36:1†	3.08:1 3.36:1
					Powerglide*	3.36:1	3.36:1
365*	Special 4-Barrel Carburetor, High-Flow Air Cleaner	11.0:1	Special Cam, Mechanical Lifters	Single, Vacuum-Centrifugal	3-Speed	3.36:1	3.36:1
					4-Speed* (2.20:1 Low)	3.70:1	3.08:1 3.36:1 3.55:1 3.70:1 4.11:1 4.56:1
375*	Fuel Injection, Special Air Cleaner	11.0:1	Special Cam, Mechanical Lifters	Single, Vacuum-Centrifugal	3-Speed	3.36:1	3.36:1
					4-Speed* (2.20:1 Low)	3.70:1	3.08:1 3.36:1 3.55:1 3.70:1 4.11:1 4.56:1

*Optional at extra cost.   †3.08:1 Performance Cruise Ratio optional at extra cost.

Corvette's hidden headlights were the first on an American production car since the 1942 DeSoto, making them fascinating fare for the day. Less appreciated, perhaps, was that neither body style offered a trunklid, so items had to be slid into the cargo compartment from behind the seats—which was far easier in the coupe (shown) than in the convertible. Powertrain choices for 1964 included four engines, three transmissions, and a host of rear-axle ratios.

1965 CORVETTE STING RAY

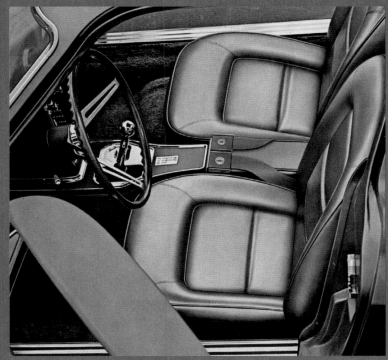

Styling changes for 1965 were subtle but defining: The hood was devoid of '64's indents, and the twin side "scoops" behind the front wheels were traded for a trio of vertical vents. Mechanical changes included the welcome substitution of four-wheel disc brakes for the previous drums.

Perhaps the most noteworthy change to the '65 Corvette didn't arrive until midyear, when the Mark IV "big-block" 396-cubic-inch V-8 replaced the fuel-injected 327, bringing an extra 50 horsepower along for the ride. The big engine was accompanied by a prominent hood bulge and side exhaust pipes to warn potential contestants of its 425-horse stampede.

THE 1966 CORVETTE STING RAY BY CHEVROLET

Features and Options and all that's new

With the introduction of the Sting Ray in 1963, Corvette adopted independent rear suspension to replace the former solid axle. It incorporated an unusual transverse leaf spring, a design that would be used in 'Vettes for many years to come. The same cannot be said for the cockpit's vertically oriented radio, which was positioned at the bottom of the center stack and would appear only in this generation of Corvettes.

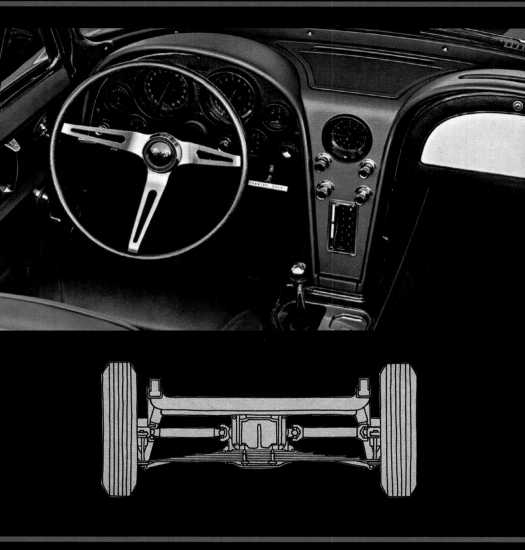

The Sting Ray ragtop outsold its coupe counterpart by ever wider margins as time passed; by 1966, the difference was almost two to one. Aside from a bigger big-block for '66—growing from 396 to 427 cubic inches—the year brought few noteworthy changes aside from a crosshatch-patterned grille to replace the previous horizontal bars, Corvette script on the hood, and, for coupes, side roof pillars devoid of vents.

Decisions, decisions. By 1966, Corvette buyers faced a daunting number of interior and exterior color choices. Most popular paint for the model year—by far—was the Nassau Blue shown on the car above. Least popular? Tuxedo Black.

EXTERIOR COLORS

Tuxedo Black   *Ermine White*   *Rally Red*   *Nassau Blue*   *Laguna Blue*

Trophy Blue   *Mosport Green*   *Sunfire Yellow*   *Silver Pearl*   *Milano Maroon*

INTERIOR VINYLS

Blue   *Bright Blue*   *Black*   *Saddle*

Red   *Green*   *Silver*   *White/Blue†*

Interiors are color-keyed to exterior colors. All (except green and white/blue) can be ordered in genuine leather seat trim.

'67 Corvette
BY CHEVROLET

Several minor styling alterations marked the '67 Sting Ray. Five shorter front-fender gills replaced the former three, and, in the rear, a horizontal back-up light appeared over the license plate frame. Big-block models got a revised hood scoop (shown), and Rally wheels (also shown) were newly available.

Optional in '67 was a 427-cubic-inch big-block V-8 with 390 ground-pounding horsepower. And that was just to start. Hotter versions were rated at 400 and 435 horses, both with Tri-Power triple two-barrel carburetors. But the monster of the pack was a wolf in sheep's clothing: the L88. Though officially rated at "only" 430 horsepower, it was rumored to put out closer to 560. Its $950 price—more than twice that of the 435-hp engine—kept all but 20 "in-the-know" buyers away.

1967 STING RAY POWER TEAMS

Engine Bore & Stroke	Horsepower & Torque at RPM	Carburetion & Induction System	Comp. Ratio	Cam & Lifters	Trans-missions	Axle Ratios	
						Standard	Positraction
STANDARD ENGINE							
327-cu.-in. V8	300 @ 5000	4-Barrel	10.0:1	General Performance	3-Speed (2.54:1 Low)	3.36:1	3.08:1 3.36:1
4.00 x 3.25 ins.	360 @ 3400	High-Flow Air Cleaner		Hydraulic	4-Speed (2.52:1 Low)	3.36:1	3.08:1 3.36:1
					Powerglide	3.36:1	3.36:1
EXTRA-COST OPTIONAL ENGINES							
327-cu.-in V8	350 @ 5800	4-Barrel	11.0:1	High Performance	4-Speed (2.52:1 Low)	3.36:1	3.36:1 3.55:1
4.00 x 3.25 ins.	360 @ 3600	High-Flow Air Cleaner		Hydraulic	4-Speed (2.20:1 Low)	3.70:1	3.70:1 4.11:1
427-cu.-in. V8	390 @ 5400	4-Barrel	10.25:1	High Performance	4-Speed (2.52:1 Low)	3.08:1*	3.36:1
4.251 x 3.76 ins.	460 @ 3600	High-Flow Air Cleaner		Hydraulic	4-Speed (2.20:1 Low)	3.36:1*	3.08:1 3.55:1
					Powerglide	3.36:1*	3.70:1
427-cu.-in. V8	400 @ 5400	Triple 2-Barrel	10.25:1	High Performance	4-Speed (2.52:1 Low)	3.08:1*	3.36:1
4.251 x 3.76 ins.	400 @ 3600	High-Flow Air Cleaner		Hydraulic	4-Speed (2.20:1 Low)	3.36:1*	3.08:1 3.55:1 3.70:1
					Powerglide		
427-cu.-in. V8	435 @ 5800	Triple 2-Barrel	11.0:1	Special Performance	4-Speed (2.20:1 Low)	3.55:1*	3.36:1* 3.70:1* 4.11:1*
4.251 x 3.76 ins.	460 @ 4000	High-Flow Air Cleaner		Mechanical			

*Available as Positraction only

Despite their exotic styling and extraordinary performance potential, Corvettes had become fairly practical and civilized beasts by 1967, thanks to available features such as leather upholstery, power windows, air conditioning, and telescopic steering wheel. And it could be dressed up even more with aluminum wheels, redline tires, and vinyl-covered hardtop. Though the standard 300-horse 327 could move the 3400-lb 'Vette with impressive authority, 70 percent of '67 models were ordered with one of the optional engines.

Back in 1967, a buyer could walk into their local Chevy dealer, add the $437 427-cubic-inch/435-horsepower V-8 and $184 four-speed manual transmission to a $4241 Corvette roadster, and end up with a $4862 land-bound missile that's worth a small fortune today. If we only knew....

C3

1968–1982

PART 1: 1968–1977

As it turned out, Corvette's shortest-running generation would be followed by its longest. The C3 took Chevy's sports car through a tumultuous time in its history, spanning the highs and lows of horsepower production and staving off extinction.

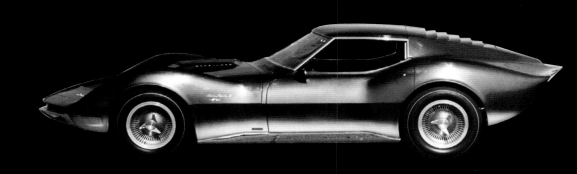

Styling for Corvette's third generation would be based on the Mako Shark II show car of 1965 (above), with pointed nose and ducktail rear capping a "wasp-waisted" profile incorporating bulging fenders and a fastback roofline. In many ways, it looked like a Sting Ray that had been stretched out like a piece of taffy. Softened curves and a tunneled rear window were seen on later design studies, both of which were adopted for production models.

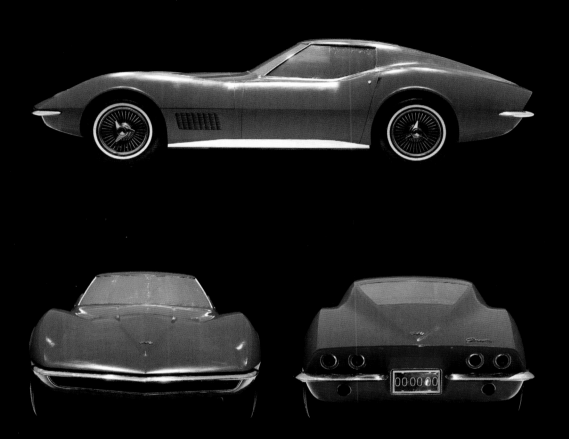

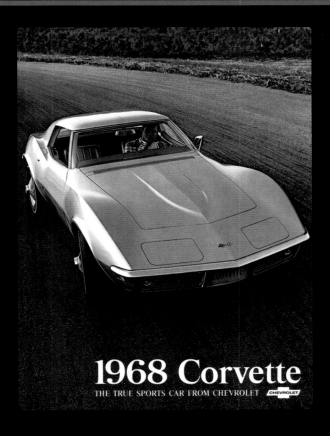

1968 Corvette

THE TRUE SPORTS CAR FROM CHEVROLET

Corvette was once again offered in convertible and coupe body styles, but with a twist: Coupes would get twin lift-off roof panels called "T-Tops," along with a removable rear window. And the name was now just "Corvette," the Sting Ray suffix having been dropped—at least for now. *Above*: Windshield wipers were concealed beneath a panel that raised when they were activated. It was a slick system, but proved troublesome.

Below: Simulated wire wheel covers were newly available for the '68 Corvette. 'Vettes with the optional big-block 427 V-8 got a revised hood bulge, but horsepower outputs were unchanged, ranging from 390 to 435. Still available was the L88 version, which was rated at only 430 hp, but probably put out upwards of 550. The secret about this engine was getting around; while just 20 were called for in 1967, 80 were ordered in '68.

Interiors were equally new, boasting space-age styling with deep-set gauges and central control panel.

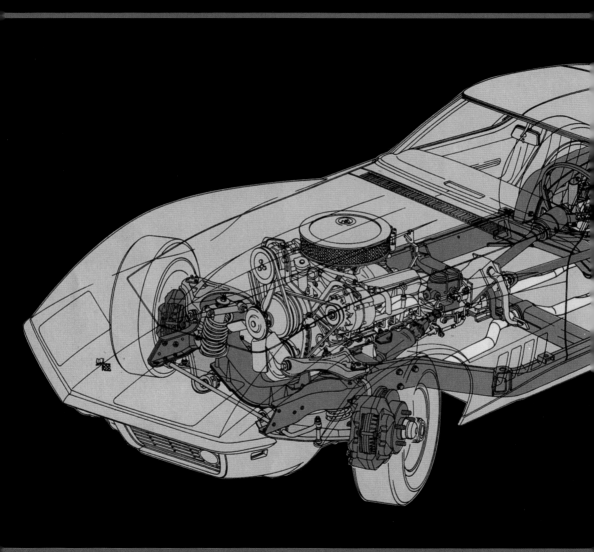

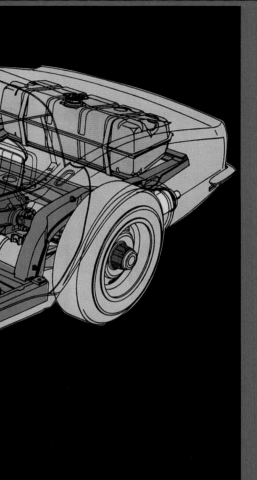

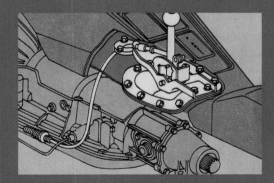

Corvette's radically new styling covered a little-changed chassis, which continued to feature independent rear suspension with a transverse leaf spring. Engine choices remained the same, but the Sting Ray's optional two-speed Powerglide automatic transmission gave way to a three-speed Turbo Hydra-Matic.

Pick a paint!

Here's a tough one. Try to select just one of these ten luxurious Magic-Mirror colors. Eight of them are brand new. (Tuxedo Black and Rally Red are popular choices we kept from last year's selection.) The fabric top for the Convertible can be specified in black, white or beige. You can also order a black vinyl cover for the removable hardtop.

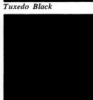
Tuxedo Black

International Blue

Silverstone Silver

Corvette Bronze

Cordovan Maroon

British Green

Polar White

Rally Red

Safari Yellow

Le Mans Blue

Among Corvette's 1968 color choices, British Green barely edged out Le Mans Blue as the most popular hue. Tuxedo Black again brought up the rear. Convertibles could get a hardtop in body color (right) or covered in black vinyl. *Opposite page*: The hood bulge gives fair warning that a 427 V-8 powers this beautiful Rally Red convertible.

1969 CORVETTE

Putting you first, keeps us first

Corvette received a surprising number of changes for 1969, but none were obvious. Again the horsepower leader—at least in official rating—was the big-block 427 Tri-Power with 435 (below). At the other end of the scale, the 327 small-block was stroked to 350 cubic inches, but put out the same 300 or 350 horsepower.

One visible change for '69 was the return of the Stingray moniker, which reappeared as one word rather than two and was placed over the front-fender gills. *Top row, left to right*: Returning options included Deluxe wheel covers, air conditioning, Positraction rear axle, and rear luggage rack. Newly available were chrome trim for the front-fender louvers and a side-mounted exhaust system that rejoined the option list after a year's absence.

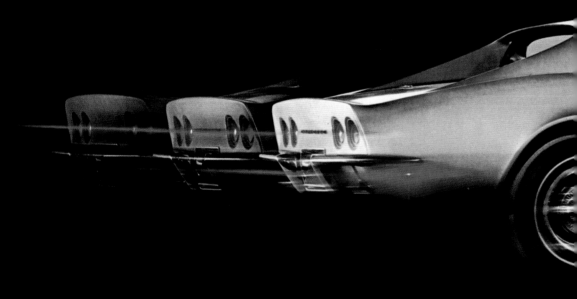

Lots of options grace this '69 convertible, including a vinyl-covered hardtop, fender-louver trim, side exhaust, and—new for '69—white-lettered tires. Beneath the hood is a 390-horse 427 mated to an automatic transmission. Nineteen sixty-nine marked a turning point in Corvette sales; not only did the production total of 38,762 top 1968's record number by more than 10,000 units (partly due to a longer model year), but the ratio of coupes to convertibles flip-flopped—and in a big way. Formerly, convertibles were always more popular, but for 1969, coupes made up 57 percent of production.

Among standard-issue Corvettes, this blazing red '69 coupe carries the year's hottest combination: 435-horsepower 427 with four-speed transmission in the slightly lighter coupe body. Only the 116 'Vettes fitted with the "Off-road application only" L88 427 with its reported 550+ hp were more potent. New this year was an all-aluminum (block and heads) version of the L88 called the ZL1, of which only two were built—partly because this engine cost as much as the car itself.

Opposite page: Because nothing quite like the Corvette has ever been produced—before this 1970 brochure or since—the headline was obviously in error. *Below:* Coupes continued to grow in popularity, attracting 61 percent of buyers in 1970.

People have the idea you can tell what cars of the future will be like by looking at Chevrolet's Corvette.

They're right.

'70 Corvette

Strength in numbers for 1970— 300, 350, 370, 390, 460 hp.

Every Corvette is built tough right from the start. Our basic V8, the 300-hp Turbo-Fire 350, features a 10.25:1 compression ratio, a 4-barrel carb, cast aluminum alloy pistons and a precision-formed crank. With this, and all other Corvette engines, you get Corvette's dual exhausts with new rectangular outlets and Positraction rear axle standard.

Go one step up to the 350-hp Turbo-Fire 350, and you get an 11.0:1 compression ratio, impact-extruded aluminum alloy pistons, finned aluminum rocker covers, a high-performance cam and a forged steel alloy crank. Our 370-hp 350 features the same hardware as the 350-hp version plus an aluminum intake manifold, domed hood, special cam, special exhaust and mechanical lifters.

Next step up. Our 390-hp 454-cu.-in. Turbo-Jet V8. This engine uses a cast aluminum alloy intake manifold, chromed air cleaner and rocker covers and an extra-large oil pan. You also get a high-domed hood, heavier duty front springs, a larger diameter front stabilizer bar, heavier duty rear wheel spindle support arms, a rear suspension stabilizer bar, a larger capacity radiator, dual pulleys for the fan and water pump and a higher performance starter motor.

Also available: our 460-hp Turbo-Jet 454 with a large 4-barrel carb, high-performance cam, mechanical lifters, aluminum cylinder heads and full-transistor ignition system.

Transmissions: standard gearbox is a floor-mounted, wide-range 4-Speed, 2.52:1 low gear. Also available, a close-ratio version with a 2.20:1 low (close ratio not available with 300-hp engine, wide range not available with 460-hp engine).

With the 300-, 390- and 460-hp engines, you can order Turbo Hydra-matic. Just sit back and let this 3-range fully automatic transmission shift for itself; or upshift and downshift through the 1-2-3 quadrant yourself with all the benefits of a stick and none of the legwork.

Chevrolet Corvette Stingray Convertible with removable hardtop.

7

Windshield wipers. Headlights. Door handles. Coupe roof panels. Everything tucks away but the landing gear.

We call the '70 Corvette "Body Beautiful." But it's also an application of pure design—the most extensively aerodynamically tested model we've ever offered.

Every facet of its design, from the front and rear spoilers to the flush-fitting door handles, has been wind-tunnel tested and refined.

For those who have trouble deciding between a coupe and a convertible, we have some alternatives. Every convertible comes with a soft top. You can order a removable hardtop, too. In the coupe model, the roof panels lift off to let the sunshine in. So, any

way you work it—you've still got a convertible feel for '70. And no matter which way you go, tinted glass is standard.

Convertible tops can be ordered in white, black or sandalwood, while a grained black vinyl roof cover is available for the convertible's removable hardtop.

For '70, there's a new grille of precision-cast metal. In the outboard corners of the grille, you'll find Corvette's new larger parking lights with their parabolic reflectors.

Complementing the change up front are new chromed louvers and new stainless steel body sill moldings on each side. The hidden

headlights come with their own washing system for the outer units. The new look in the rear includes high-visibility taillights and rectangular exhaust extensions.

You'll also notice a flare to the wheelwells on the '70 Corvette for extra body protection from flying stones and debris from the road. Standard tires are F70 x 15 wide-ovals mounted on 8-in.-wide wheels. This combination makes for the best traction, handling and tire mileage characteristics ever offered on Corvette. You can opt for your choice of white lettering or white stripes, too.

Chevrolet Corvette Coupe with roof sections removed.   11

Corvette got some revised engines for 1970. Added to the 350-cubic-inch small-block family was a potent LT1 version making 370 horsepower. Total sales amounted to just 1287. Also offered was a big-block newly enlarged from 427 cubic inches to 454, an LS7 version of which produced a mighty 460 hp. Total sales? Zero. Zip. Nada. Why? Though listed in ads and brochures, apparently the engine couldn't be made "smog legal" and had to be canceled. A shame.

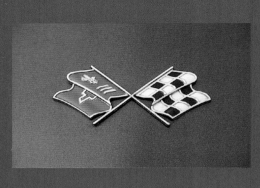

In the absence of the 460-horsepower LS7 454 that never materialized, the 390-hp LS5 version became 1970's top dog. Other changes for the year included square front turn signal lenses mounted in an eggcrate grille, "mesh" front-fender gills, and rectangular dual exhaust tips.

Corvette
1971 Stingray Coupe/Convertible

Engine	Transmission	Ratio Without Air Conditioning			Ratio With Air Conditioning		
		Std.	Optional		Std.	Optional	
			Econ.	Perf.		Econ.	Perf.
Base engine							
270-hp (210-hp†) 350-Cu.-In. Turbo-Fire 350 V8	Turbo Hydra-matic	3.08	—	3.36	3.08	—	3.36
	4-Speed (2.52:1 low)	3.36	3.08	—	3.36	3.08	—
Available engines							
330-hp (275-hp†) 350-Cu.-In.(RPO LT1) Turbo-Fire 350 V8	4-Speed (2.20:1 low)	3.70	3.55	4.11	Air Conditioning Not Available		
	4-Speed (2.52:1 low)	3.55	3.36	3.70			
365-hp (285-hp†) 454-Cu.-In.(RPO LS5) Turbo-Jet 454 V8	Turbo Hydra-matic	3.08	—	3.36	3.08	—	—
	4-Speed (2.20:1 low)	3.36	3.08	3.55*	Air Conditioning Not Available		
	4-Speed (2.52:1 low)	3.08	—	3.36	3.08	—	—
425-hp (325-hp†) 454-Cu.-In.(RPO LS6) Turbo-Jet 454 V8	Turbo Hydra-matic	3.08	—	3.36	Air Conditioning Not Available		
	4-Speed (2.20:1 low)	3.36	3.08	3.55			
	Special 4-Speed (2.20:1 low)	3.36	3.08	3.55**			

†SAE net (as installed) horsepower rating. *Special 3.70 ratio also available. **Special 3.70 or 4.11 ratio also available.

Chevrolet **Putting you first, keeps us first.**

Nearly all cars for 1971 had engines with lower compression ratios that allowed them to run on the newly available unleaded fuel, but it also allowed them to produce less horsepower. Furthermore, power ratings were to switch from "gross" to lower "net" ratings for '72, so some manufacturers included both in their specifications. On the positive side, 1970's stillborn LS7 454 finally materialized with lower compression as the LS6, producing 425 gross horsepower, or 325 by the new net rating.

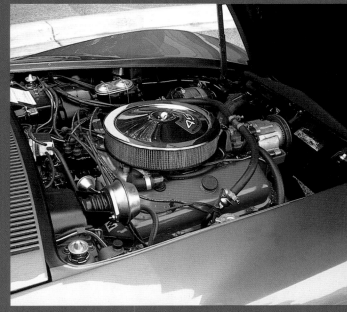

A rare bird indeed is this 1971 Corvette with the ZR2 package, as only 12 were built. The package included heavy-duty brakes and suspension, a mandatory four-speed manual transmission, and the LS6 425-horsepower 454 fitted with transistorized ignition. A similar ZR1 package was available with the LT1 350 small-block, now rated at 330 hp. ZR1s are rarer still, as only eight were built.

Sports car buyer's guide:
1972 Corvette

CHEVROLET

Few appearance changes marked the 1972 Corvettes, though Ontario Orange (pictured at left) vaulted from fourth place to first in the color race. Pewter Silver (above) brought up the rear. The '72s were noteworthy as being the last Corvettes to have chrome bumpers front and rear, and in coupes, a removable back window.

It was beneath the skin that '72 'Vettes changed the most, as engines took a horsepower hit—and not just from the new "net" ratings. Tightening emissions regulations took their toll, sucking 10 net horsepower from the standard 350 (to 200), and 55 hp from the lone 454, now rated at 270. Perhaps due to fears things would only get worse, sales climbed nearly 25 percent to 27,000.

Our Corvette Coupe
has two removable roof panels.

The convertible's folding top is standard. The hardtop is well worth the price.

Corvette was still offered in coupe and convertible form, but coupes were growing ever more popular, accounting for 75 percent of sales in 1972. Not coincidentally, orders for optional air conditioning were also on the rise. Coupes still came standard with removable T-tops, while convertibles continued to offer an optional lift-off hardtop.

One of the few ways to tell a '72 from a '71 is by the yellow (rather than clear) front turn signal lenses. The cars were otherwise so similar that Chevrolet mistakenly used a clear-lens '71 in its 1972 brochure (see page 149), the license plate starting with "OOP" perhaps being a bit prophetic.

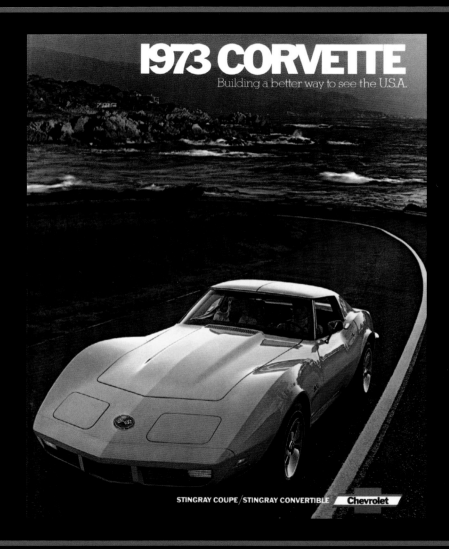

1973 CORVETTE

Building a better way to see the U.S.A.

STINGRAY COUPE / STINGRAY CONVERTIBLE **Chevrolet**

The 1973 Corvette was unique in combining the '72 rear end with a new front end that incorporated a government-mandated five-mph bumper. Most cars adopted big ugly beams to meet the requirement, but many felt Corvette's urethane-covered bumper actually improved its looks. It was joined by front fenders with side scoops rather than the previous grilles. Horsepower ratings fluctuated only slightly, with the 350 small-block at 190 or 250 horsepower, the 454 big-block at 275.

BUILDING A BETTER WAY TO SEE THE U.S.A. **Chevrolet**

For 1974, rear bumpers also had to meet the government's five-mph requirement, and Corvette's did so with a urethane-covered one similar to that used in front the year before. And again, it looked far better than most. This style would continue for many years, but the '74 version was unique in being molded in two pieces, with a "split" down the middle; later versions were one piece.

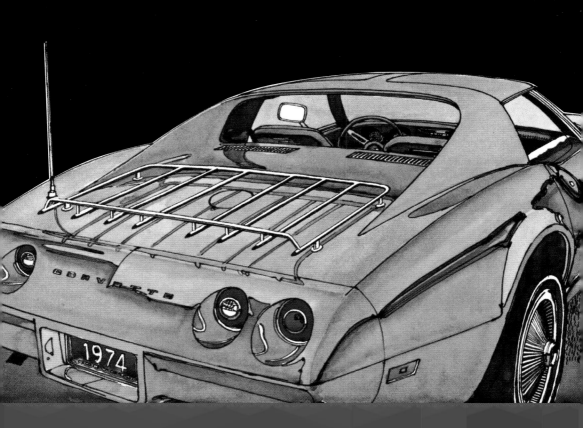

Horsepower ratings again changed little, but 1974 would prove to be the final year for the 454 big-block. Corvette sales increased again, as did the percentage that were coupes. Also on the rise were the percentage that had the base engine, automatic transmission, and air conditioning, indicating a buyer preference that was increasingly favoring luxury over sheer performance.

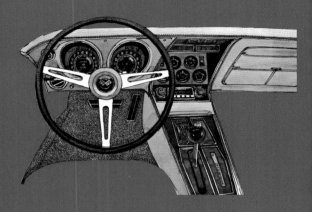

While interiors didn't change much, the features ordered for them did. The popularity of Custom Interior Trim (which included leather upholstery and woodgrain accents) and power windows were both escalating, and the '74 brochure mentioned that dual resonators had been added to the exhaust system, because its growl "seemed to be too prominent." All this served as further testament that Corvette buyers were increasingly outfitting their cars as plush *Gran Turismos* rather than performance-oriented sports cars.

Convertibles made their final appearance in 1975, falling victim to both buyer apathy and proposed federal rollover standards. With the big-block V-8 relegated to history, the top engine option became the L82 350 with 205 horsepower, 40 more than the base L48 version.

CORVE

'75

TTE

Chevy's small-block V-8 celebrated its 20th year in 1975, and it had been the standard Corvette engine for 19 of them. Starting at 265 cubic inches and 195 horsepower, it hit its peak during the C2 generation, with fuel-injected 327s putting out as much as 375 hp. Emissions standards and lower net horsepower ratings had dropped the top version to just 205 hp by 1975 (probably about 260 by the old gross method), but the small-block had many more years—and a lot more power—left in it.

Despite being less expensive, convertibles attracted just 12 percent of Corvette buyers in their swan song year. It would be more than a decade before a new 'Vette could once again drop its top. The cost of meeting federal safety and emissions standards was taking its toll on prices, with the 1975 convertible going for $6550, while the coupe was $6810.

1976 Corvette

CHEVROLET

The little-changed 1976 Corvette came only in coupe form, carried a much higher price...and set a new sales record. The standard 350 V-8 (commonly known as the L48) added 15 horsepower for a total of 180, while what Chevrolet called the "Special V-8" (what everyone else called the L82) gained five for a total of 210.

For Corvette's 1976 production run of more than 46,000 units, the most popular color was white, followed by silver, red, and dark brown. Only 22 percent of buyers chose a manual transmission, and only 12 percent opted for the higher-powered L82 engine. Newly optional were eight-slot aluminum wheels.

The only one.

Corvette by Chevrolet.

Chevrolet

In a year that saw few other changes, 1977 introduced some new options. Ordering the tilt/telescopic steering column brought a sporty three-spoke steering wheel (above). Glass canopy roof panels could replace the standard body-colored one, which could now be strapped to the available rear-deck luggage carrier (right).

Engines choices for 1977 remained the standard 180-horsepower L48 350 or the optional 210-hp L82 version. The standard Rally wheels (opposite page) could be replaced by optional eight-slot aluminum rims (below), first offered in '76. Despite a $1000 price hike to $8647, sales set another new record, topping 49,000.

C3

1968–1982

PART 2: 1978–1982

Corvette entered its tenth year as a Shark with little more than a new roof contour, celebrating its 25th anniversary with paint-and-trim packages. Prices that had been merely escalating were now skyrocketing, yet sales of Chevrolet's sports car only dipped with word that the long-promised fourth generation was waiting in the wings.

For those familiar with the Corvette's early struggle to stay alive, celebrating its 25th anniversary must surely have been a joyous occasion.

The Silver Anniversary Corvette

All 1978s were considered 25th Anniversary models, but special Silver Anniversary Paint (light silver over dark silver, shown above) was a popular option chosen by nearly a third of all buyers. Biggest change to the Corvette for 1978 was the "glassback" roofline that replaced the channeled buttresses used before.

Not only did the new design provide better rear-corner visibility, it also allowed easier access to the cargo compartment. Inside, a restyled dashboard placed the round main gauges in rectangular pods, a three-spoke steering wheel was made standard, and a proper glovebox was added in place of the former vinyl map pocket.

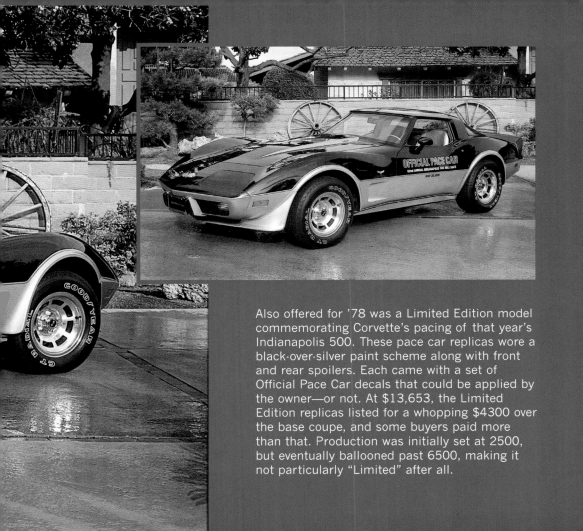

Also offered for '78 was a Limited Edition model commemorating Corvette's pacing of that year's Indianapolis 500. These pace car replicas wore a black-over-silver paint scheme along with front and rear spoilers. Each came with a set of Official Pace Car decals that could be applied by the owner—or not. At $13,653, the Limited Edition replicas listed for a whopping $4300 over the base coupe, and some buyers paid more than that. Production was initially set at 2500, but eventually ballooned past 6500, making it not particularly "Limited" after all.

After a 1978 model year that included a major styling revision along with two special-edition packages, the little-changed '79s promised to be a bit of a letdown. But buyers evidently didn't see it that way, snapping up 53,807 of them—a new record, and one that still stands. Power got a bit of a boost, the base L48 engine now rated at 195 horsepower, the L82 at 225. In a rather unusual shift in color popularity, black (which had not been offered at all from 1970 to 1976, and often brought up the rear before then) vaulted into first place—by a wide margin—attracting nearly 20 percent of buyers.

Front and rear spoilers that first appeared on the 1978 pace car replicas became molded-in features for 1980. Air conditioning was newly standard, as were power windows, but that hardly justified a near $3000 price increase to $13,140. By the end of the model year, it stood at $14,345. Not surprisingly, sales were off significantly from record 1979 levels.

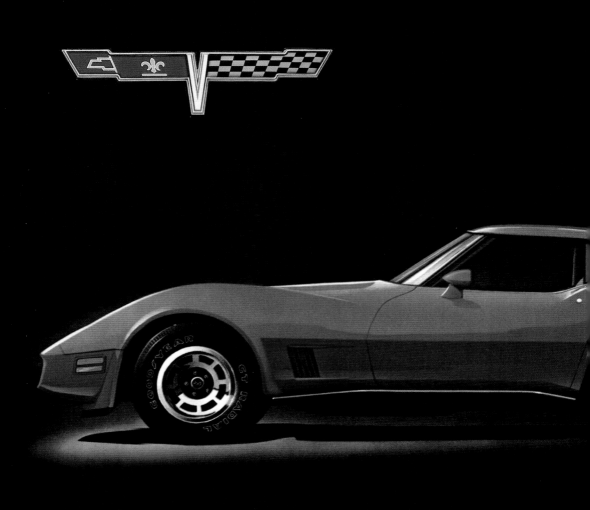

For 1980, the base L48 engine lost five horsepower, now 190, while the L82 gained five, for 230. Due to stricter emissions regulations in that state, California buyers had to make do with a 180-hp 305-cubic-inch V-8 that came only with automatic transmission— as did almost all the L82s. A new crossed-flag emblem graced the Corvette's nose, and nearly 85 percent were fitted with the optional slotted aluminum wheels (shown).

1981

Top and lower right: Corvette's molded, body-colored bumper caps spared it the ugly "girders" worn by most cars to meet the federal five-mph impact standard. For 1981, the underlying support structures were changed from steel to fiberglass, as was the transverse rear leaf spring (in red at lower left). Combined, the switch saved more than 100 pounds. Also for '81, the previous L48 and L82 engines gave way to a single L83 with 190 horsepower—up five over the L48, but down 40 (ouch) from the L82.

During the 1981 model year, Corvette production moved from St. Louis to a new plant in Bowling Green, Kentucky. A high-tech paint facility allowed the use of large-flake metallics, and four two-tone combinations were added to the palette.

cross·fire·injection

Ever-tightening emissions standards challenged engineers, and for 1982, Corvette adopted Cross-Fire Injection to become the first "fuelie" Vette since 1965. The twin throttle-body injectors looked somewhat like carburetors and were mounted diagonally on each side of a broad intake manifold. Cross-Fire's higher level of sophistication added 10 horsepower, now an even 200. In another "retro" move, the four-speed manual transmission was dropped, meaning that for the first time since 1954, all Corvettes came with automatic.

Chevy makes good things happen... for you

Chevrolet

Corvette closed out the long-running C3 generation with a specially trimmed Collector Edition. This layout from the 1982 brochure boasts of its "Unique silver-beige metallic paint, pin stripes and fading shadow treatment...distinctive cloisonne emblems...specific wheels...and special Vehicle Identification Numbers." But perhaps its most significant feature was a flip-up glass rear window—unique to the Collector Edition—that greatly eased access to the luggage compartment.

C4

1984–1996

PART 1: 1984–1990

Few cars have been more fervently rumored and eagerly anticipated than the fourth-generation Corvette. Skipping the 1983 model year—and thus its 30th anniversary—the C4 was introduced to great fanfare and glowing accolades. It signaled a turnaround in the Corvette's mission, once again stressing "sport" over "luxury."

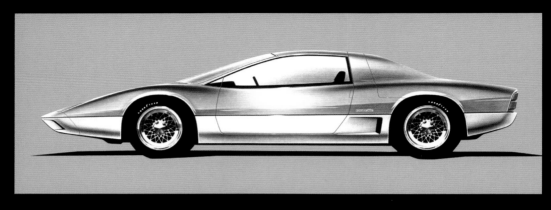

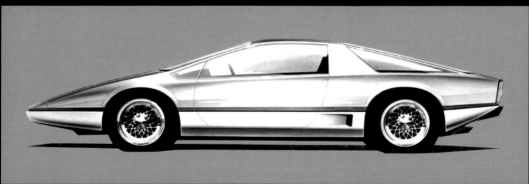

This page: Concept sketches from the mid 1970s that predated the actual C4 development program assumed a midengine layout for the next-generation Corvette. While seriously considered and widely encouraged, the midengine concept proved too costly to produce. *Opposite page:* A 1979 mock-up shows both a traditional front-engine design and a close resemblance to the finished product.

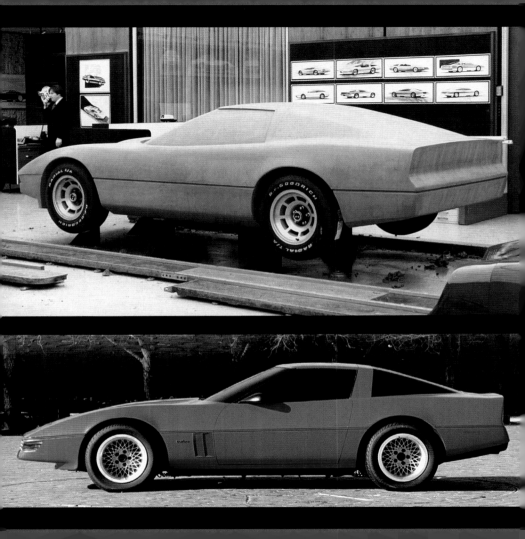

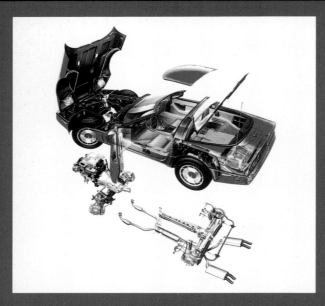

Practicality was obviously given consideration in the design of the C4. The flip-up rear glass opened to a large cargo well between the seats and the fuel tank, and a forward-tilting clam-shell hood granted access to the entire front end of the car. The roof was removable, as in the C3, but the opening was devoid of the T-top's center bar. The Cross-Fire Injection 5.7-liter V-8 carried over from '82, but now with 205 horsepower vs. 200, and it came standard with a four-speed automatic transmission. Much to the satisfaction of enthusiasts, a four-speed manual returned after a one-year hiatus, now with overdrive in the top three gears. This resulted in seven speeds, and the name "4+3."

Perhaps the most controversial element of the C4 was its digi-graphic instrument panel. Designers were striving for a hi-tech look, and they got it—though traditionalists yearned for round, analog gauges.

Despite an entirely new look, the C4 was instantly recognizable as a Corvette, having retained such features as round taillights and a chiseled, tapered snout. Standard equipment included 16-inch "turbo-vane" cast-aluminum wheels. Among the options was a race-bred Z51 Performance Handling Package that brought stiffer springs along with wider wheels and tires.

Arriving in March 1983 gave the '84 an 18-month "model year" that helped it achieve Corvette's second-highest production total: 51,547. Three new shades of "champagne" were offered, but red was by far the most popular color.

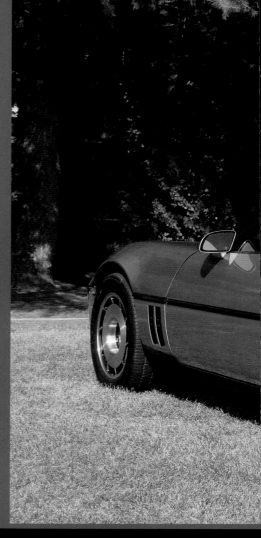

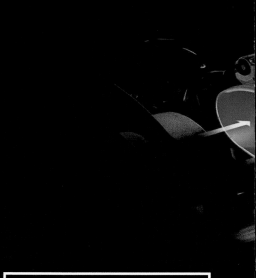

Replacing the Cross-Fire Injection L83 for 1985 was the new Tuned-Port Injection L98. Both engines displaced 5.7 liters, but the revisions brought 25 more horsepower for 230 total, along with a cool-looking intake plenum with ram-horn feeding tubes. According to Chevrolet's figures published in Corvette brochures, the new engine dropped the 0-60-mph time with the four-speed manual from 6.4 seconds to just 5.7, while top speed rose from 142 mph to 150.

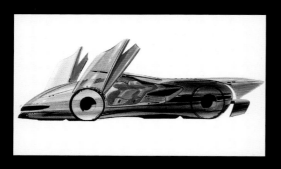

Dreams of a midengine 'Vette still danced in Chevrolet's head during the 1980s. Design work for what became the Corvette Indy concept car began in 1984, with a running prototype appearing two years later. The hi-tech stunner featured all-wheel drive, four-wheel steering, and a backbone frame made largely of carbon fiber. But like other midengine dreams before it, the Indy idea was shelved due to high costs.

After more than a decade without one, the Corvette got a convertible variant for 1986, an event that was celebrated by fans and factory workers alike. Ragtops were built on the same Bowling Green line as their coupe counterparts.

In its triumphant return, the convertible garnered 20 percent of Corvette sales, a popularity it hadn't enjoyed since 1972. Making this feat all the more impressive was that in a reversal of earlier custom, the convertible now cost more than the coupe—by a lot: $32,032 vs. $27,027. A number of minor changes occurred for 1986, including the adoption of standard antilock brakes and a high-mounted third brake light, the latter mandated by law.

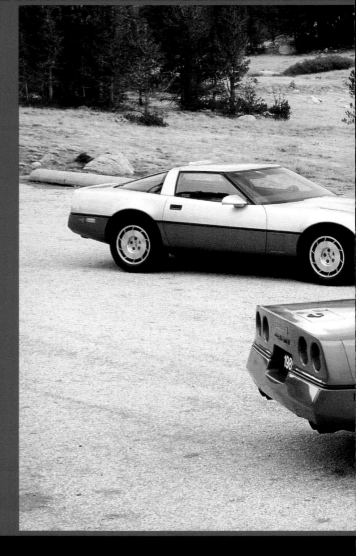

A newly minted Corvette convertible paced the 1986 Indianapolis 500 under the able guidance of famed test pilot Chuck Yeager. While all 1986 Corvette convertibles were considered pace car replicas—and came with decals to prove it—the actual pace car was yellow, as were 732 of the production versions.

For 1987, Corvette's horsepower rating inched up to 240, thanks to roller rocker arms and 1986's optional aluminum heads, which were now standard. Newly available was the Z52 suspension package. It added some elements of the high-performance (and hard-riding) Z51 suspension to the base setup, resulting in a ride/handling balance that many thought was "just right."

Convertibles accounted for more than a third of Corvette production for 1987, a year in which Bright Red was by far the most popular color. A Callaway Twin Turbo engine package became a regular production option. Cars so ordered were drop-shipped from the Bowling Green factory to Callaway in Connecticut, and when finished, sent to the ordering dealer. The twin-turbo engine was rated at 345 horsepower.

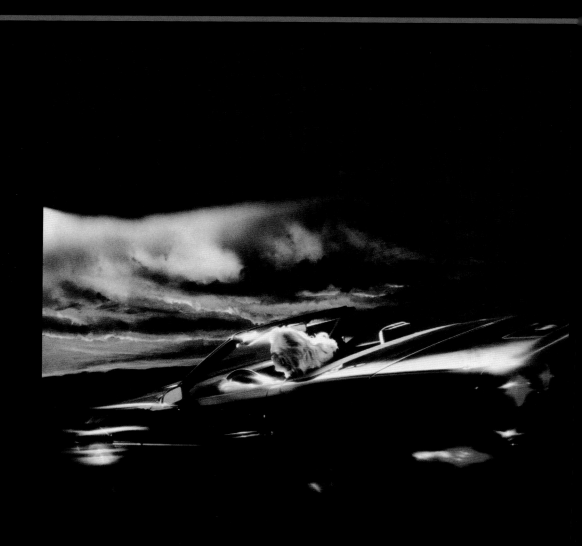

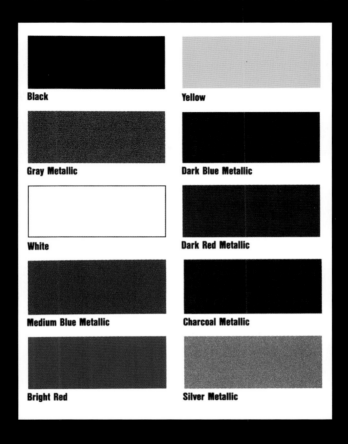

Black

Yellow

Gray Metallic

Dark Blue Metallic

White

Dark Red Metallic

Medium Blue Metallic

Charcoal Metallic

Bright Red

Silver Metallic

What color is the Corvette of your dreams? The palette was
down to ten choices for 1988, the most popular again being
Bright Red, followed by white and black.

New six-slot 16-inch wheels (shown) were standard on Corvettes for 1988. By this time, sales were down to about half of 1984's record of 51,000, settling in the mid to low twenties where they'd stay through the end of this generation. Once again, convertibles made up more than a third of production.

A 35th Special Edition Package was offered on 1988 coupes. All were painted white with black tops and had a white-and-black interior along with unique trim and badging. The white wheels were painted versions of new 17-inchers offered as an option on other Corvettes. Only 2050 anniversary editions were sold—partly because the package cost nearly $4800.

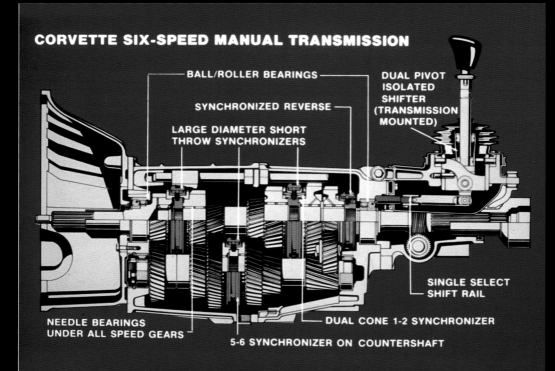

CORVETTE SIX-SPEED MANUAL TRANSMISSION

BALL/ROLLER BEARINGS

DUAL PIVOT ISOLATED SHIFTER (TRANSMISSION MOUNTED)

SYNCHRONIZED REVERSE

LARGE DIAMETER SHORT THROW SYNCHRONIZERS

SINGLE SELECT SHIFT RAIL

NEEDLE BEARINGS UNDER ALL SPEED GEARS

DUAL CONE 1-2 SYNCHRONIZER

5-6 SYNCHRONIZER ON COUNTERSHAFT

228

Opposite page and above: A new six-speed manual transmission built by ZF of Germany replaced the 4+3 Doug Nash unit for 1989. The ZF included a feature called CAGS (Computer Aided Gear Selection) that forced the shift lever from first gear to fourth under light acceleration. The intent was to improve fuel economy enough in the EPA city cycle to avoid a Gas-Guzzler Tax, which it did. C4 convertibles finally got an optional hardtop late in the 1989 model year.

This page: In its biggest change since inaugural 1984, the C4 got a rounded, cockpit-style dashboard design for 1990. A digital speedometer sat in the center of the instrument panel, but most other gauges were dials—though not the round ones favored by enthusiasts. *Opposite page:* The 17-inch wheels that had been optional in 1988 became standard for '89; both of these 1990 convertibles are wearing them.

While only a handful of production cars were faster than a standard-issue Corvette, Chevrolet wanted to cut that to a mere thimbleful. Enter the ZR-1. What quickly became known as the "King of the Hill" was introduced in 1990 as a $27,000 option package that nearly doubled the price of a base coupe. External differences were limited to wider rear flanks (to cover massive 11-inch-wide rear tires), a convex rather than concave rear fascia, rectangular taillights vs. round, and subtle ZR-1 badges. But that's not where the money went.

Under the ZR-1's stock-looking hood lay the heart of a monster: a state-of-the-art, all-aluminum, 5.7-liter double-overhead-cam V-8. Called the LT5, it was designed by Lotus, built by Mercury Marine, and produced 375 horsepower—a whopping 50 percent more than the standard L98, which was no wimp itself. Though docile as a lap dog in traffic, it turned ferocious when it bared its fangs: Testers recorded 0-60-mph times of under five seconds and a top speed of 175 mph. At left is a 1989-model prototype that was shown to the press. Note the rear bumper's "LT5" badge, which was replaced by "ZR-1" on production models.

C4

1984–1996

PART 2: 1991–1996

With the C4 generation looking to run for several more years, Chevrolet gave it a midcycle styling update— and soon after, a healthy increase in power. They made the Corvette a better car, but the combination served to silence the guns of the mighty ZR-1.

1991

Rounded extremities marked the Corvette's 1991 update. The front end took on a sleeker, more aerodynamic appearance, and if the new tail generated a sense of déjà vu, it should: The rectangular lights and bulbous contour mimicked the look of the ZR-1, making that exotic seem just a little less "special." Also for '91, wheels were restyled with "shark fin" vanes, and front-fender vents wore horizontal strakes in place of the previous vertical gills.

More changes came for 1992, primarily in the form of more power. Several revisions to the V-8 unleashed 50 more horses for a total of 300 and prompted a new name: LT1. Actually, the name itself wasn't new; it had been used in the early '70s on a high-performance version of the small-block. Standard for '92 was Acceleration Slip Regulation, a traction-control system that tire-smokers of the world were relieved to find included an "off" switch. *Opposite page, top left:* Possibly due to the horsepower increase on regular 'Vettes, sales of the exotic (and expensive) ZR-1 package plummeted from 2044 in 1992 to just 502 for '93.

July 2, 1992, saw a milestone car roll off the Bowling Green assembly line. The one-million-
lionth Corvette was a white-over-red convertible, just like the original '53. *Opposite page:*
Several GM dignitaries were on hand to give the millionth 'Vette a resounding thumbs-up.
Among them were two prominent chief engineers: the C4's David R. McLellan (second from
right), and long-retired Zora Arkus-Duntov (far left), who breathed life into early Corvettes
and was likely amazed that both he and the sports car GM nearly killed in the mid 1950s
would live to see this day.

There were few changes to standard-issue Corvettes for 1993, but there was one new option: a passive keyless-entry system, sometimes referred to as "proximity locks." A keyfob in pocket or purse would automatically unlock the doors as the driver approached the car, and lock them as the driver departed.

With the LT1 closing in on horsepower, the ZR-1 got a much-needed infusion of 30 more ponies for 1993, bringing the total to 405. The car pictured wears the 40th Anniversary Package offered on all Corvettes that year, which included Ruby Red paint and leather upholstery, along with special trim and badges. Despite the extra power, ZR-1 sales continued to decline, dropping to just 448.

Corvettes added a passenger-side airbag for 1994, but could no longer be ordered with cloth upholstery. Air conditioning systems switched to new R-134a refrigerant, and convertibles got a glass rear window with defroster. New to the options list were Goodyear Extended Mobility Tires—what are now called "run-flats." Copper Metallic (shown) was a new color choice, but was only applied to 116 cars. ZR-1s got exclusive new five-spoke wheels for 1994, but no other changes of note. Production matched 1993 output at 448.

A Corvette paced the Indianapolis 500 for the third time in 1995, and about 500 replicas—all convertibles—were duly offered to the public. (The actual pace car, shown in brochure above, was also a convertible, but fitted with a roll bar for safety's sake.) They couldn't be missed on the street, as vivid graphics augmented a purple-over-white paint scheme. *Opposite page, bottom:* After a predetermined run of 448 examples, Chevy closed the curtain on the ZR-1. Sales had never met expectations; the original goal was 4000 to 8000 per year, but over its six-year life, total production reached only 6939.

For 1996, a new 330-horsepower LT4 engine was fitted to six-speed cars, while automatics kept the 300-hp LT1. The swan song season of the C4 generation saw coupes selling for $37,225, convertibles (which accounted for 20 percent of production) for $45,060.

Two special-edition models marked the end of the C4 generation. The Grand Sport (this page) was intended to evoke the '60s racing Corvette of the same name. It came only in Admiral Blue with white center stripe and a pair of red slash marks on the left front fender. Coupes rode on the same five-spoke wheels as the departed ZR-1, but they were painted black, and the massive rears were covered by fender extensions. Convertibles used the same style of wheel but in conventional Corvette size. All Grand Sports had the 330-horsepower LT4 engine and six-speed manual transmission. Only 100 were built. More common—at 5412 units—was the Collector Edition (opposite page), with Sebring Silver paint and silver five-spoke wheels.

CHAPTER 6

C5

1997–2004

With the C4 growing long in the tooth from its 13-year run, Chevrolet brought forth a curvacious, state-of-the-art successor that maintained the Corvette heritage while upping the ante in the sports car sweepstakes.

Designer: Randy Wittine
Sculptor: Gary Clark

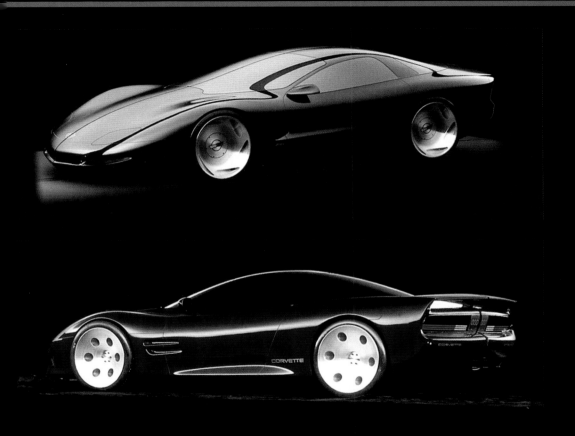

The low, tapered nose found on some early concepts would surely have been unreasonable for production, but rounded edges and a return to "wasp-waisted" styling would prove prophetic.

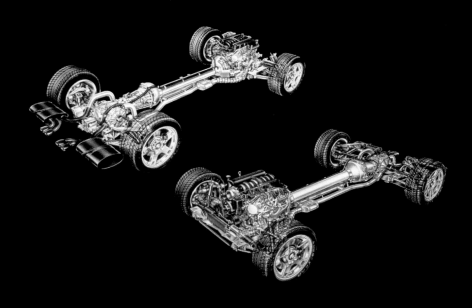

While a midengine layout remained too costly to justify, a mid-mounted transmission apparently was not; it was fitted just ahead of the differential. The engine and transmission were connected by a substantial driveshaft housing, and the design resulted in an almost perfect front/rear weight balance. *Right:* The Corvette design team poses with a near-final C5 mock-up.

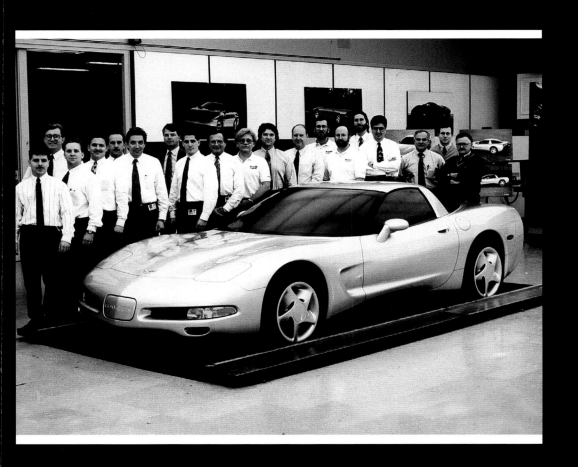

THE NEW CORVETTE.
YOUR WILDEST DREAM
STARTS RIGHT NOW.

For many enthusiasts, this brochure's brash headline was no exaggeration. The C5 exhibited a level of style, sophistication, and outright performance that awed longtime fans and attracted new ones.

A clean-sheet redesign of Chevy's classic small-block V-8 resulted in the all-aluminum LS1. Lighter than the iron-block LT1 and LT4 engines it replaced, it produced 345 horsepower, 15 more than the potent LT4 version. A four-speed automatic transmission was standard, but driving through the optional six-speed manual, the new LS1 could pull a 'Vette from 0-60 mph in a blistering 4.7 seconds.

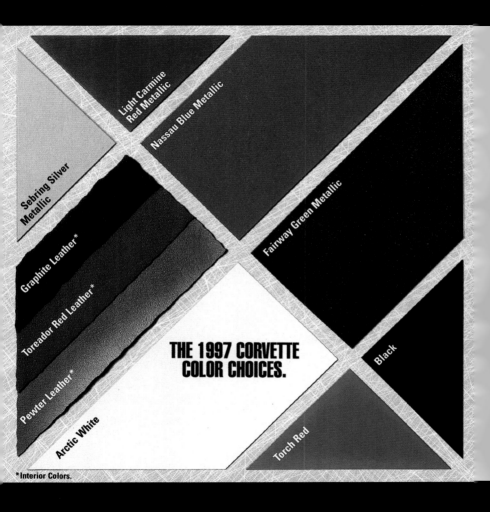

Light Carmine
Red Metallic

Nassau Blue Metallic

Sebring Silver
Metallic

Graphite Leather*

Fairway Green Metallic

Toreador Red Leather*

**THE 1997 CORVETTE
COLOR CHOICES.**

Black

Pewter Leather*

Arctic White

Torch Red

*Interior Colors.

After a one-year hiatus, a convertible returned to the lineup for 1998. It was the first Corvette ragtop since 1962 to have a trunklid for easier cargo access. Though 1997 sales amounted to just over 9700 due to production limitations, the Bowling Green assembly line cranked out 31,084 Corvettes the following year—including 11,849 of the new convertibles.

A Corvette convertible was chosen as pace car for the 1998 Indianapolis 500, marking the 'Vette's fourth appearance at the Brickyard. Deep purple paint was set off by striking yellow wheels, a colorful graphics package, and yellow-trimmed interior. Chevy sold 1163 virtually identical replicas to the public.

For 1999, Corvette added its first-ever hardtop body style; unlike the coupe, it had no removable roof panel, essentially being a convertible with a fixed top. It came out lighter and stiffer than its companions, and was thus sold as a performance model. It came standard with the Z51 Performance Handling Package and six-speed manual transmission, both of which were optional on other Corvettes. However, it didn't sell as well: just 4031 vs. 18,078 coupes and 11,161 convertibles.

2000 C5 CORVETTE PRODUCTION CAR

2000 C5-R CORVETTE RACE CAR

Left: What would grow into the highly successful C5-R racing program began in 1999 at the Rolex 24 Hours of Daytona. A C5-R placed third in the SCCA's United States Road Racing Championship GT2 class. *Above:* A switch to the American LeMans Series (ALMS) in 2000 brought third- and fourth-place finishes in the GTS class. It also brought a change of colors. Though highly modified, the C5-R was a production-based racer, and Corvette promotions stressed its similarity to street cars, which gained new slim-spoke wheels for 2000 (top).

2001

The hardtop (foreground) realized its performance potential in 2001 as Chevrolet transformed it into the Z06. A new LS6 V-8 gave it 35 more horsepower than the parent LS1 engine, which itself was up to 350 horsepower for 2001. Also unique to the Z06 were wider twin-spoke wheels.

After placing second and third in the 2001 ALMS 12 Hours of Sebring, the number 3 and 4 Corvette C5-Rs went on to dominate the GTS class, winning eight of the ten races they entered. The C5-R also claimed its first of four consecutive ALMS GTS Manufacturer's Championships in 2001.

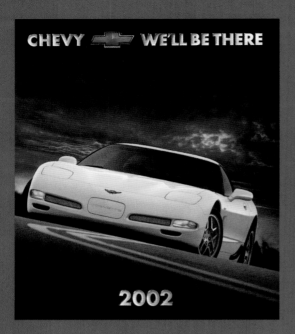

CHEVY ✨ WE'LL BE THERE

2002

Corvette coupe and convertible changed little for 2002, but the Z06 hardtop (background) added another 20 horsepower, bringing the total to 405. By this time, the Z06 was the most expensive car in the lineup, and the first to top the $50,000 barrier. Nonetheless, sales jumped significantly to 8297, while total Corvette production reached 35,767.

With its newfound power, the Z06 managed to eclipse the performance of its "King of the Hill" predecessor, the exotic—but heavier— 1990–95 ZR-1. Testers managed 0-60 mph in the low-four-second range, the quarter-mile in about 12.8. A "405 Horsepower" badge on the front fender differentiated the '02 from an '01.

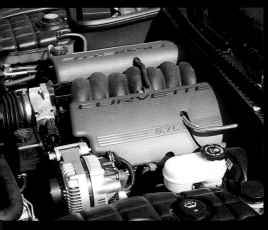

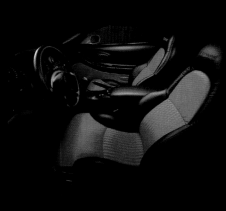

In a fitting tribute, a 2003 50th-Anniversary Corvette was chosen to pace the 2002 running of the Indianapolis 500 before the 2003 models had even been introduced to the public. This time, no special pace car replica was issued, though a pace car graphics package could be purchased.

Corvette celebrated its 50th anniversary for 2003 with a special trim package for the coupe and convertible (it wasn't available on the Z06). It included Anniversary Red paint, gold-tinted wheels, unique emblems, and a two-tone beige interior that brought the C5's first nonblack dashboard. (The dash had gained round dials and a convenient layout with the C5 redesign.) The $5000 package was ordered on 32 percent of coupes and 54 percent of convertibles, which outsold coupes for the first time since 1968.

For the 2003 running of the 24 Hours of LeMans, Chevrolet commemorated its 2001 and 2002 wins by eschewing the C5-R's traditional yellow paint in favor of LeMans Blue with silver and red stripes. A similar color scheme was offered on 2004 production Corvettes in a Commemorative Edition Package (opposite page, lower left). When applied to a Z06, the package included a carbon-fiber hood. The C5-R just missed a class win in 2003, but scored a first and second in the '04 24 Hours of LeMans. The second-place number 63 car—once again wearing its traditional yellow paint—is shown searing its brakes entering a turn. Also in 2004, a Corvette paced the Indy 500 for the sixth time (left).

CHAPTER 7

C6

2005–2013

With the C6 generation, Chevrolet built on the already-impressive C5 by giving it tidier dimensions, more horsepower, and less weight—a surefire formula for greater performance. And perform it did, even before the advent of the revived Z06, which set standards few cars in the world could match.

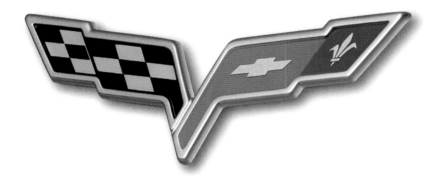

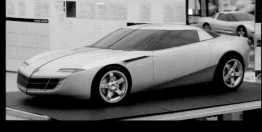

Early styling studies for the C6 kept classic Corvette proportions and most wore some form of side scoops or gills, but little else was held sacred. Among these many studies, few styling elements can be seen that eventually made it to production.

Another round of clays brought the C6 closer to its final form. Rooflines, side scoops, and front and rear treatments that eventually appeared in production models can be seen in these images.

Whereas the C5 ended its reign with three body styles, the C6 would start out with two. Chassis layout retained the front-engine/rear-transmission layout, along with Corvette's now traditional transverse leaf springs. The engine was changed enough to warrant a new designation: LS2.

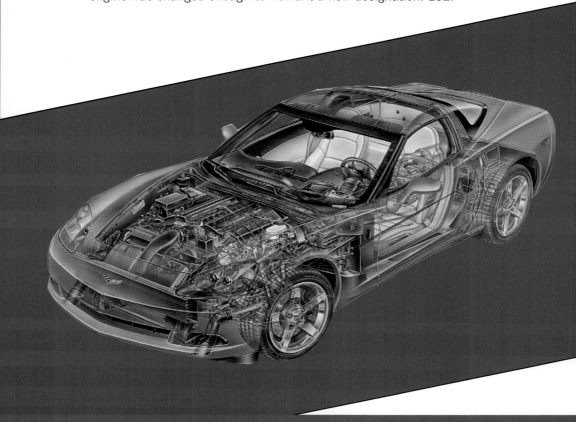

A bore increase boosted displacement to 6.0 liters (from 5.7), bringing with it a corral of extra ponies, up from 350 horsepower to 400. A six-speed manual transmission was standard, with a new six-speed automatic optional.

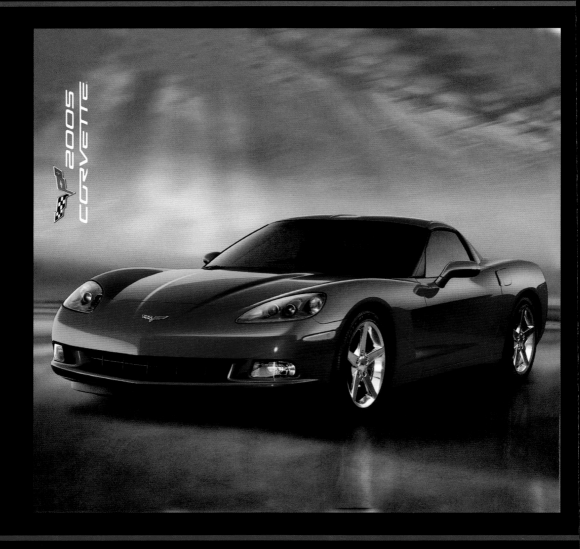

2005 CORVETTE

400hp

While the C6 retained many C5 styling elements and was easily identifiable as a Corvette, it broke the long-standing tradition of hidden headlights. Instead, the lights were placed under clear covers that conformed to the front fender lines. Brochures trumpeted power and performance improvements.

4.2 0-60

Convertibles offered an optional power top that raised or lowered in less than 20 seconds. When stowed, it was hidden beneath a hard, body-colored tonneau cover. A C6 convertible was given the honor of pacing the Indy 500 in 2005.

Like the C5 before it, the C6 went racing. Its competition debut came at Florida's famed 12 Hours of Sebring in March 2005. After leading for much of the race, the two factory C6.Rs were involved in accidents, yet still managed to finish second and third in the American LeMans Series' GT1 class—an impressive showing for an all-new car. But that was just a warm-up. The team dominated the rest of the season, taking the GT1-class win in all 10 remaining races, placing first *and second* in nine of them, earning Chevrolet the manufacturer's championship.

After a one year hiatus, Chevrolet unleashed a C6-based Z06. It was worth the wait. Developed in concert with the C6.R, the '06 Z06 carried many racing-inspired pieces, including an aluminum chassis structure, carbon-fiber front fenders, and a magnesium engine cradle, all contributing to significant weight savings. *Below:* Perhaps not surprisingly, a Z06 was chosen to pace the 2006 running of the Indy 500. It marked the third time in three years and the eighth time in history that a Corvette had been enlisted for that duty.

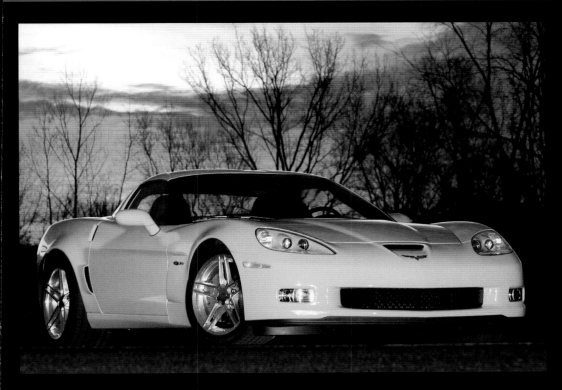

A Z06 can be readily identified by its front-mounted air scoop, brake-cooling ducts at the leading edges of the rear wheelwells, red-colored brake calipers, and flared fenders that cover wider front and rear wheels (the 12-inchers in back are three inches wider than stock). Inside, there's unique trim. But the real star of the show resides under the hood: a highly modified small-block V-8 stretched to 7.0 liters. For those with an appreciation for history, it measures 427 cubic inches—same as the big-block V-8s of the 1960s. Output is a stupefying 505 horsepower. Testers clocked 0-60-mph sprints in under four seconds, with a top speed approaching 200 mph.

Opposite page: The Z06 introduced what was essentially a third body style, that being the coupe with a fixed roof panel to aid body stiffness. Note the "double bubble" roof, a styling element found on both the Z06 and targa-top coupe. *This page:* A $64,890 Z06, $43,690 coupe, and $51,390 convertible unleash a com-bined 1300 horsepower in a pavement-pounding stampede. Lesser sports cars should run for cover, because the Bad Boys from Chevrolet are coming to town.

CHAPTER 8

C7

2014–2019

"America's Sports Car" entered its 61st year with a dramatic, edgy redesign that brought to mind the beauty of Corvette's past—including the first Stingray in 40 years.

The C7 maintained the basic layout and proportions set by the C5 and C6. But the latest Corvette was all new and shared almost nothing with the C6. Heightened performance, dramatic styling, improved interior quality, and increased use of high-tech materials helped secure the future, while the return of the Stingray name invoked Corvette's past. Chevy's all new "Gen 5" small-block V-8 debuted with the 2014 Stingray's LT1 engine. The 6.2-liter mill was good for 455 horsepower in base form, making it the most powerful standard Corvette engine so far.

Three-dimensional Stingray logos decorated the front fenders of the 2014 Corvette Stingray, whose aggressive, creased design was a departure from the smoother styling of the C6.

Corvette Racir
preserved the
silhouette of t
(above). Even
C7 'Vettes
benefited from
sportier touch
like Stingray-
emblem whee
left) and a 7-s
Tremec manu
gearbox with
smoother shif
(near left).

Z06's bodywork was revised to cover wider tires, and tweaked aerodynamics helped generate downforce to improve grip and stability (above). The heart of the C7 Z06 was the new LT4 V-8 (right), a supercharged 6.2-liter engine good for 650 horsepower—eclipsing C6 ZR1's "mere" 638.

The Z06 was now also offered as a convertible (above), and for the first time it could be ordered with an automatic transmission: a new 8-speed with paddle shifters. A Z07 Performance Package (left) added more aerodynamics, carbon-ceramic brakes and even stickier Michelin tires.

The Jet Black Suede Design package shown here included red-striped black wheels, red brake calipers, a black hood graphic, black badges, and a rear spoiler. The interior was finished in sueded black microfiber.

The 2016 Z06 C7.R Edition was inspired by Corvette Racing's black-and-yellow color scheme and styling, so exterior color choices were limited to the new-for-2016 Corvette Racing Yellow or black. Sections of the hood and ground-effects package were finished so the carbon-fiber pattern remained visible. All had black interiors with yellow detailing and carbon-fiber trim.

On March 1, 2016, Chevrolet introduced the 2017 Corvette Grand Sport at the Geneva International Motor Show in Switzerland. The Grand Sport was essentially a Z06 powered by the Stingray's naturally aspirated 460-horsepower 6.2-liter LT1 V-8. Grand Sport was offered in all Corvette colors, and front-fender hash-mark stripes or full-length bodytop stripes in a variety of colors could be added. The Grand Sport Collector Edition shown here was different. It only wore the exclusive color Watkins Glen Gray Metallic, named for the famous New York track. Tension Blue hash marks, black satin stripes, and black wheels finished the purposeful look. The headrests were marked with an embossed rendering of an original 1963 Grand Sport racer.

In November 2017, Chevrolet introduced the 2019 ZR1 coupe at the Dubai Motor Show, and quickly followed it up with a convertible variant unveiled at the Los Angeles Auto Show. The new model boasted a supercharged 755-horsepower LT5 6.2-liter V-8. Buyers could choose a seven-speed manual or eight-speed automatic transmission. Chevy claimed a ZR1 equipped with the automatic was capable of 0-60 mph times of less than three seconds and quarter-mile runs in the high-ten-second range. With the standard "Low Wing" rear spoiler, the ZR1 had a claimed top speed of 212 mph. There was also a ZTK Performance Package that included an adjustable "High Wing" rear spoiler, but this aerodynamic setup resulted in a lower top speed. The 2019 Corvette ZR1 coupe's base price was $119,995, while the convertible started at $123,995.

CHAPTER 9

C8

2020–

The C8 generation was a radical departure from the traditional Corvette design. After experimenting with the mid-engine layout for 60 years, Corvette introduced a midengined production car.

The late Zora Arkus-Duntov was the godfather of the Chevrolet Corvette during its early years and pushed for a production midengined 'Vette in the Seventies. The Aerovette prototype came close to production for 1980, but Chevrolet decided to continue with the conventional front-engine Corvette instead. Duntov's dream of a midengined Corvette was finally fulfilled for 2020. The mid-engine layout has long been the norm for exotic supercars and with its eighth-generation car, Corvette joined the club. The C8 debuted with a 490/495-horsepower 6.2-liter V-8 and Chevy claimed it would go 0-60 mph in less than three seconds with a top speed of 194.

Even faster additions to the line were expected after the C8's rollout. In spite of its exotic-car specs, the new Corvette Stingray coupe started at a reasonable $59,995. A convertible with a retractable hardtop was also available. Plus, there was a CR.8 racecar based on the new 'Vette to compete in the International Motor Sports Association's GTLM class.